The Circle
of Hanh

BOOKS BY BRUCE WEIGL

POETRY

Executioner (1976)

A Sack Full of Old Quarrels (1977)

A Romance (1979)

The Monkey Wars (1985)

Song of Napalm (1988)

What Saves Us (1992)

Lies, Grace & Redemption (selected poems and an interview,
edited by Harry Humes, 1995)

Sweet Lorain (1996)

Not on the Map (with Kevin Bowen,
edited by John Deane, Dublin, 1997)

Archeology of the Circle (new and selected poems, 1999)

After the Others (1999)

TRANSLATION

Poems from Captured Documents (translated from the Vietnamese
with Thanh Nguyen, 1994)

Mountain River: Vietnamese Poetry from the Wars: 1948–1993
(translated from the Vietnamese and edited
with Nguyen Ba Chung and Kevin Bowen, 1998)

Angel Riding a Beast, poems by Liliana Ursu
(translated with the author, 1998)

CRITICISM

The Giver of Morning: On Dave Smith (1993)

The Imagination as Glory: The Poetry of James Dickey
(with T. R. Hummer, 1994)

Charles Simic: Essays on the Poetry (1996)

ANTHOLOGY

Writing Between the Lines: An Anthology on War and Its Social Consequences
(with Kevin Bowen, 1997)

The Circle of Hanh

A Memoir

Bruce Weigl

Grove Press/New York

Published simultaneously in Canada
Printed in the United States of America

FIRST EDITION

Library of Congress Cataloging-in-Publication Data
Weigl, Bruce, 1949–
The circle of Hanh : a memoir / Bruce Weigl.
p. cm.
ISBN 0-8021-1661-2
1. Weigl, Bruce, 1949– . 2. Poets, American—20th century
Biography. 3. Vietnamese Conflict, 1961–1975—Veterans—United
States Biography. 4. Vietnamese Conflict, 1961–1975—Literature and
the conflict. I. Title.
PS3573.E3835Z464 2000
811'.54—dc21
[B]   99-40263
CIP

DESIGN BY LAURA HAMMOND HOUGH

Grove Press
841 Broadway
New York, NY 10003

00 01 02 03   10 9 8 7 6 5 4 3 2 1

for Peter S.

Contents

Acknowledgments

A version of "The Borderline" appeared originally in *American Poetry Review* and a version of "Spike" appeared originally in *The Ohio Review,* to whose editors I am grateful.

I am also grateful for the support of my friend Toby Thompson, who helped show me a way to tell my story; to Larry Heinemann for his friendship and his good writer's eye; to Reg Gibbons for the same; to Morgan Entrekin, Eric Price, and Ellen Levine for their generosity of spirit and for their belief that I could write this book; and to Andrew Miller, who found a shape for my story.

And the saviors who are fast asleep
they wait for you . . .
—Bob Dylan

The Circle
of Hanh

Prologue

I want to resurrect something ancient from inside me because I was not raised to be a man who cares for words as if they were living things. From birth, I headed in a direction away from books. I've always felt most at ease digging some kind of hole, or carrying something heavy for low wages. In the grim apartments and the small houses where I grew up among working-class people—immigrants and the children of immigrants—there were no books.

This is not a confession, except in the way all stories confess. This is a journey to uncover the story of how I arrived at where I am and who I am. I have forgotten a great deal. I've lost track of too many details. I've lost whole years to drugs and to that long, black postwar grief.

I don't know how it all happened. I'm not even sure I want to remember everything. I don't believe remembering everything is necessary for our happiness or well-being. Some things need to stay buried deep. I have only a story and my belief in the ability of stories to save us.

Once I was a small boy among people who loved me as best they could. My mother was kind and she cared for me. She washed and mended with great care the clothes my older cousins passed down to me. She combed my hair with a black rattail comb dipped in a jar of green gel that made my hair wave up straight like a hedge.

She worried for me when I'd be out past the time I was due home in a way that made me feel cared for and wanted.

My father would hold me on his lap when he came home from the mill. He would smell of slag, although I knew he had already washed the black grit off before he came home. He'd take another bath at home, and afterwards, while my mother cooked his supper, he'd come into the kitchen in his white T-shirt and clean blue work pants and take a bottle of beer from the fridge. He'd sit down at the kitchen table and talk to my mother as she stood at the stove.

One year for Christmas he bought a used bicycle from my uncle and took it downstairs to the dark basement we shared with the others who lived in our apartment building. He told me that autumn not to go down into the basement. He said there were rats down there that he'd have to take care of. He wanted to hide the bicycle from me while he tried to build it back into something shining. He worked many long nights after coming home from the mill to rebuild and paint the bike. He straightened the dented fenders and painted them red. With his sure hand he painted a thin white stripe along the fender's edge. He put new tires on the bike and a new seat. He polished the handlebars and shined a mirror he found somewhere.

On Christmas morning when I ran out of bed into the living room where our small tree was lit up, the first thing I saw was the bike. It was the most beautiful thing I had ever seen in my life. It didn't matter to me that it wasn't new. Outside, snow swirled in the cold Ohio December but I wanted to ride my new bike. My father carried it down the apartment's stairs to the street past my mother, who insisted it was too cold outside to ride a bike, and too dangerous in the ice and snow. I followed him down, wearing my winter coat over my pajamas. He let me ride the bike down the driveway and then down the street for half a block where the snow had been plowed away.

Sometimes when I misbehaved, when I did something wrong to my sister or talked smart (as he called it) to my mother during the day, my father hit me with his belt when he came home. He'd hit me until I cried, or until my mother came in the room and made him stop. Maybe he hit me with the belt out of love, because always afterwards he'd call me to sit in his lap where he would hold my face close to his neck. I smelled the soap there, and the father-smell of beer and cigarettes that I loved, and the sting from the belt would fade.

My people worked hard for long hours and when they came home they were usually too tired to play; sometimes they were too tired even to talk. Because they seemed so tired to me, and because I loved them, I played mostly by myself, although I didn't understand that I was lonely. I would lose myself in a vacant lot next to our apartment that seemed to me then like a vast wilderness, an undiscovered country I imagined could be mine. I sang songs to myself but I don't remember the tunes or the words anymore. I imagined them as working songs. In my country of weeds that grew above my head, with brambles so thick they could hold a boy down, I wanted to work like my people. I sang my working songs, and with a blade I made from a flat piece of steel I found in the rubbish, I cut the weeds I imagined as food I could give my mother and my father. I cut the dried weeds and stacked them in bundles that I tried to tie together with string.

I made a small house there too, from some boxes and boards I found behind St. Peter's Catholic Church next door. I covered the house with the dried weeds and brambles so no one could find me. I took leftover food from our kitchen when no one was around and stored it in my house. I took dried onions and garlic that my grandmother had grown in her garden, and hard apples from my uncle's farm. I knew it was wrong to take the food. I was afraid my mother would catch me. I was afraid of the belt. I didn't know what I was doing. I think now that I must have found some kind of life there inside of a story that sustained me.

The one day of my country of weeds and cardboard house stretched into the many days of my childhood until I came to see my far, vast territory of weeds and brambles as only a vacant lot next door, and the weeds and brambles as only weeds and brambles that someone had forgotten or was too lazy to mow. My house fell apart in the rain one day; it rotted and then disappeared under the shoes of other neighborhood children who had come to play there. I had to give up my country, but the story stayed inside me. The story sustained me. And the next day, I was grown.

We had no money for college and I wasted any athletic potential I may have had on my dreaminess. I took my chances in the Army. One day towards the end of my senior year in high school, with nothing going for me except maybe a mill job or a low draft number, an immaculate Army recruiter came to speak to the assembled at Admiral Ernest J. King High School.

I knew nothing about Vietnam. Although it was 1967 and the antiwar movement was already becoming something real and even dangerous, it wasn't a struggle that had reached us yet in Lorain, Ohio. I didn't pay much attention to the soldier who came to my school, outside of the gorgeous perfection of his uniform, which seemed to beckon to me. I didn't listen to him until I heard him talk about how the Army would pay for me to go to college after I'd done my duty, and although I knew nothing about college either, and had wasted my high school career, I knew that I wanted out of Lorain.

Prologue

We dreamed of being heroes as teenage boys, and war was our vocation. We played war games that got so real one of my friends took a BB in the eye and couldn't see straight for months. I don't know why we were so restless and in such need of violence; as the sons and grandsons of immigrants—Serbs, Slovaks, Poles—we longed our whole lives to get out of there. We swore we wouldn't become like our fathers, punching the card in and out every day until the grit built up in the cracks of your face and your back was bent forever. We drank beer and roamed the city aimlessly in loud cars. I spent half of my life back there in those cars, cruising the drive-ins, shouting a kind of love young men practiced from a distance to women we could never have, chipping in when a buck and a half of gas would last all night, edgy, restless, crazy to be something we could not name.

I never imagined I'd end up in a war. I saw a free ride and had been well prepared to climb aboard one if it came my way. My timing, as it turned out, was bad. 1967–68 represented the last big American push to win the unwinnable war. Johnson and McNamara had sent upwards of 500,000 troops to Vietnam by then. If you had a warm body, you were in. My body was hot.

I graduated high school in June and by December I was in An Khe, the Republic of South Vietnam, and with the 1st Air Cavalry I gradually moved north towards trouble of such dimensions that the most powerful army in the history of warfare would be brought to its knees.

The paradox of my life as a writer is that the war ruined my life and in return gave me my voice. The war robbed me of my boyhood and forced me, at eighteen years old, to bear too much witness to the world, and to what men were capable of doing to other men, and to children, and to women, and to themselves, trapped in the green inscrutable intention of the jungle.

The war took away my life and gave me poetry in return. The war taught me irony: that I instead of the others would survive is ironic. All of my heroes are dead. The fate the world has given me is to struggle to write powerfully enough to draw others into the horror.

I ended up north on Highway One past Hue. I must have drunk some bad water from the Ca Lu River because I got sick. I shit and I vomited, and in my stomach a black snake grew. They sent me to base camp at An Khe where I slept in twisted sheets on a cot until a man from the Red Cross threw a book at me from a box of books and said *Read this boy*.

<O>

That morning as I lay sick on a cot, holding the paperback, I could not say the names that I read there, even out loud to myself. I had been born into the house of my working mother and father, the house of no books, but I kept reading, the dream of the suffering horse pulling me in. I read Raskolnikov's letter over and over. Something snapped into place in my brain.

"I fear in my heart that you may have been visited by the latest unfashionable unbelief," Pulcheria wrote to her son.

I don't know why the words made sense to me then: 1968, the war raging all around us, the air filled with screams. The world must have conspired to put me there, in that war, in that province of blood, at that moment, so the man could drop that book on my bunk without looking at me. That book was my link to another world, my bridge to a space blown wide open with a light that filled my brain.

Prologue

I ran away from the steel-mill town and its grit to the war. I was not headed in the direction of books, but there was a moment while I read and reread *Crime and Punishment* that morning, my stomach raw from bad water, my nerves blown out, my life on a wire, when I must have glimpsed the enormous possibilities of expression because I remember that I was jarred from one way of thinking into another.

At that moment, the enormity and the impossibility of the struggle at hand revealed itself as a kind of splendor or order that vanished as quickly as it appeared.

I have looked for that enormity ever since. It has become my way to find it in the darker corners where it wants to weld something hurtful to something human. I come from a long line of violence. In my life that's left I want to find a shape for the litany of terror to bring it into comprehension. The impossible and terrible beauty of our lives: that we use them up, that the hunger fades.

What endures is the story. The story circles back on itself if you let it have its way, and if you care for the words as if they were living things whose care your own life depends upon, because it does.

Twenty years after I first stepped through that portal, the story led me back into the green everlasting jungle where I had always belonged. I let the story have its way and it circled back on itself into the lives of far away people who had never stopped calling to me. It led me back to the circle of Hanh.

Part One
The River Where
the Moon Falls

I

The circle of the story is nearly complete today, Thursday, October 19, 1996. I'm in the Noi Ba Hotel, twelve kilometers from Hanoi and five hundred yards from the Noi Ba Airport. I am almost comfortable enough with my fate to write this all down.

Much to the delight of the hotel staff who have seen many like me come and go quickly, I've renamed this place the "No Visa Hotel" because this is where the airport security people put travelers who arrive at the airport without a proper visa until they can be put on the next available flight to Hong Kong, Kuala Lumpur, Singapore, Bangkok; anywhere, as long as it is out of Hanoi, out of Vietnam.

In spite of a large sign inside the airport that said VISA ISSUED HERE, there were no visas issued at the Noi Ba, not ever.

I was escorted to the hotel by two Vietnamese friends: the poet Pham Tien Duat, who served as a soldiers' poet in the Army of North Vietnam during the long war against the Americans, traveling up and down the Ho Chi Minh Trail, writing and reciting poems for the soldiers; and Nguyen Quang Thieu, a young poet and novelist who, during the war, was a child living in the same village he lives in today, not far from Hanoi. Thieu had become one of the most important writers of the post-1975 generation. Also present was Lady Borton, a writer, activist and field coordinator for the American Friends Service Committee in northern Vietnam.

Our official escort was an airport security officer who seemed uncomfortable with his task. I know now that he was aware they would force me to leave; he saw that I had a few well-known and highly regarded friends from Hanoi and this contradiction made him uneasy. He was polite to me, even kind when he told me I could not leave the hotel grounds without a visa. When I asked him who would stop me if I did try to leave, he seemed perplexed and asked my Vietnamese colleagues why I would want to leave after he told me I couldn't. I didn't want to make him any more uncomfortable so I told him I was joking. He laughed out loud, clearly relieved, slapped me on the back, and left.

But I've gone too far ahead. I should begin this part of the story with my arrival and attempted departure from Hong Kong this same morning.

2

I arrived in Hong Kong via Seoul via New York's JFK Airport at 12:30 P.M. Hong Kong time, after more than eighteen hours of flying. My connection to Hanoi, a short flight of only an hour and a half, wouldn't depart until 2:45 P.M. and I was relieved to have a few hours to get my boarding pass, collect myself for the journey ahead and get some rest. I cleared customs quickly and set out to find the Cathay Pacific desk.

The River Where the Moon Falls

Following signs in English, I came around a corner to a wild mob scene. The hallway, about fifty feet long, was crammed with hundreds of people, mostly Asians: Vietnamese, Chinese, Japanese, Korean and Thai, all talking loud and fast and at the same time. Mid-October in Hong Kong is not unlike mid-July in Georgia, and without air-conditioning or fans, the hallway was like a sauna. Even my Asian fellow travelers, more used to the heat than I, were wiping the sweat from their brows and fanning themselves with their tickets and official papers.

It took a few minutes to realize that what had first appeared to be a random coming together of people crammed into the long hallway was actually a line. Without cutting in I tried to make my way to the front of the line to see what was holding things up and if I had to wait, as the others seemed to be doing, only to get my boarding pass. At the end of the hallway I rounded another corner to find one more hallway crammed with people. Because I am tall even in my own country, I could see over the crowd to the end of this second hallway, where I could make out the Cathay Pacific sign hung above a long counter. There were nine stations at the counter; at each station, separated from the mass of noisy travelers by a counter and a glass barrier, a Chinese man or woman stood coolly handling those fortunate enough to have made it to the counter, travelers who each seemed to have endless questions.

As I watched for a few minutes trying to decide what to do, I got lost for a moment in the confusion at the counter and in my brain. I let my mind go where it would, and it took me with an almost jarring inevitability to the day two years earlier when my wife and I had finally decided to adopt a Vietnamese child.

I could see the moment as clearly as if I were inside it, and I could feel the weight of that decision as it had felt that day: a joyful and terrifying weight, a promise made to a child who, although she had remained unknown to us for almost two years, could never be betrayed now. I remembered my sense that once we had taken that first step towards her by agreeing that we wanted to do this, there would be no turning back no matter what. I remembered our long wait while the adoption service tried to find a child they felt was a good match. After the first six months we thought it would never happen. I grew more and more impatient as I imagined this girl-child in an orphanage somewhere in northern Vietnam. I had traveled to the North many times since the late 1980s, first as a curious and frightened veteran trying to find the boy I had been in the war—to find what it was I imagined I had left there—and then as a writer and translator of Vietnamese poetry. I had visited more than one orphanage, and although they were better than one might expect—clean, and sometimes even happy with the voices of children singing—they were also frighteningly poor and understaffed. I could tell that sometimes the children did not have enough to eat.

During the months we had waited to hear from the adoption service, I would lie awake at night and picture those places, and imagine the girl. I was restless and sometimes angry at the agency for not moving more quickly, and I blamed them for the meals she would miss, the cold nights she would spend, simply because they wouldn't allow me to go to Vietnam and bring her home.

I had been fortunate enough to make many close and loving friends in Vietnam, especially in and around Hanoi, where I spend most of my time while there. They were mostly writers who were also veterans of the American and the French wars, and they provided me resources that even the Hanoi office of the adoption agency didn't have. Writers in Vietnam are highly regarded and usually well connected both socially and politically.

I decided to ignore the agency's advice to stay out of the process, and called on some of those friends for help.

I wrote a series of letters to people who were connected to the ministry that could help me in Hanoi. Less than a month after I'd given the letters to a friend who was traveling to Hanoi, my wife called me at my university office. She was at home with the social worker, who had with her a picture of an eight-year-old girl. My wife told me over the phone that the social worker wanted to know if we would adopt her. I hung up and drove wildly home. When I arrived, the social worker was getting ready to leave; she was handing my wife the dossier with the girl's story and pictures. She was telling my wife and then me as I came in the door to take our time, to think carefully after we'd read the dossier.

I looked at Jean and we both looked at the social worker and I said we didn't have to wait. Jean was holding a small photograph of a tiny girl dressed in a pink flowered pajama outfit. Although she was fighting not to smile, she was as pretty as a river where the moon has fallen.

3

A man pushing me from behind brought me back to the desk among my anxious fellow travelers. I looked towards the row of faces behind the glass and chose one I thought might help me. I approached a woman clerk but she said, "You'll have to wait your turn."

I excused myself as well as I could and interrupted her, saying I'd be happy to wait but that I simply needed a boarding pass for my flight to Hanoi, and only wondered what line I should be in.

She pointed to the mass of people milling around in front of the counter. I knew that mass spilled into the second hallway, which connected to the first hallway with its own population of weary travelers.

"That line," she said.

When I tried to ask her another question she smiled, dismissed me with a not unfriendly wave of her hand and turned to the man before her who was waving a handful of papers.

I made my way back down the two hallways to the end of the line, which had already grown longer by twenty or thirty people. I looked at my watch. It was 1:00 P.M., and though the line seemed to hardly move at all, I still felt I'd have no trouble making my flight as it didn't depart for another hour and forty-five minutes.

I settled into the line, which did not advance but got longer. I spread my bags out to make a nest and sat down on them like the many others around me. A Chinese man next to me smiled his approval and offered me a cigarette. He lit my cigarette with a Zippo lighter and flicked it shut all in one motion the way they do in American movies. I inhaled deep and smiled back at him.

He asked in English where I was going and said, "Oh, very bad place" when I told him Hanoi. I wasn't up for that conversation, so I shook my head half yes and half no and turned as if to look in my backpack.

My new friend wouldn't have it. He had shared his cigarettes with me, and he had lit me up with his Zippo and now he felt I owed him some English practice.

"Hanoi is Comoonist," he said.

I told him I wasn't a politician, and that I wasn't going to Vietnam for political reasons—partly a lie—but that I was going to adopt an eight-year-old girl from an orphanage in northern Vietnam.

My friend turned to a woman next to him whom I took to be his wife. He must have told her what I had just told him because his wife looked at me, smiled and half bowed her approval.

My friend frowned at her.

"Why you want Vietnamese girl," he said.

"Why not," I answered.

He laughed. "Hanoi is Comoonist," he said. "No good, girl from there."

The line suddenly lumbered to its feet like an elephant and moved five or six short steps down the hallway before coming to a full stop again. When I settled back down, I managed to put some people between me and my friend. He waved at me once he'd settled too, and he shook his head. Since it was so noisy you had to shout to be heard, he mouthed the words *Hanoi is Comoonist* once more so I could read his lips, and turned away.

4

Two years earlier, looking at the picture of Nguyen Thi Hanh that my wife held and reading the vital statistics of the little girl's life, I had imagined a river that ran straight from my door across the thousands of miles to her side. I had imagined that nothing could stop me from bringing her into our lives. Waiting in line, I resolved that this otherworldly airport scene would not deter me from that task. I felt a sudden, sharp loneliness sitting there with all those other people, and I longed to be at Nguyen Thi Hanh's side in Binh Luc, Nam Ha Province. I looked ahead at the sloppy line and down at my watch. Nothing would stop me from getting to Hanoi today and to Binh Luc tomorrow for my daughter.

I practiced the Buddha's first meditation and moved with the line when it moved.

There were only thirty-five minutes left before boarding when I finally reached the desk, but I could see the gate from where I stood, and I could not imagine that I wouldn't make the flight. Even if approval took longer than I thought it would, I told myself, once they found out at the desk that I held a ticket for the Hanoi flight, they'd hold the plane for me. I was almost there.

I presented my papers—passport with Vietnamese visa, stamped inside by the Vice-Ambassador himself forty-eight hours earlier, and Cathay Pacific/Air Vietnam ticket—to a Chinese woman behind the glass barrier. She smiled at me, took my documents and began to process them.

Then she stopped suddenly in such a way that I knew some great impossibility was about to overtake me, and that there was nothing I could do to prevent it.

She frowned at me, openly, glaringly, and said, "Please, wait one moment." She walked away from the counter to speak to another Chinese woman whom I saw almost immediately shake her head as she listened to what the counter woman had to say. I looked down at my watch; five more minutes had gone by.

The counter woman returned and said without emotion, "I'm sorry, we cannot issue you a boarding pass to Hanoi because your visa has expired."

I was relieved because I knew she had to be wrong, and since she was wrong it was something we could fix. With twenty-five or thirty minutes left, there was still plenty of time.

"That's impossible," I said. "I was only issued the visa two days ago by Vietnam's Vice-Ambassador to the United States in Washington, and I've been traveling for twenty-four hours."

"Your visa expired yesterday," she said, and handed my passport back to me through the small opening in the glass.

"I was only issued my visa yesterday," I said, "'that's impossible."

"Look at the date," she said, and told me to stand to the side so others could approach the counter.

I found the visa and strained to read the ink-stamped seal with the dates of issue and expiration. I knew she had to be wrong. But she wasn't. I saw that the expiration date was in fact yesterday, and that perhaps in his haste to get the visa to me in time, the Vice-Ambassador or one of his aides had reversed the issue and expiration dates so the visa actually indicated that it had been issued thirty days in the future and expired on the day it was issued. I panicked for a minute after looking at my watch: no more than twenty minutes until the scheduled departure, and I worried that they were issuing too many boarding passes, given the number of travelers already gathering at the gate.

I approached the counter woman again when I could find an opening and said, "See, there's been a mistake," but she waved me off.

"I'm sorry, there's nothing we can do. The date of expiration shows that the visa has already expired."

"But can't you see that it's a mistake," I said, "that they've reversed the two dates?"

"We are instructed to issue boarding passes for Hanoi only to those passengers traveling with a valid Vietnamese passport or with an official and legal visa from the People's Republic of Vietnam. I'm sorry," she said, "you'll have to get another visa."

I saw the opening in the mass of people leading to the departure gate get smaller.

"Where can I get another visa to Vietnam?" I asked.

"Perhaps you can get one here in Hong Kong, or perhaps in Singapore, or perhaps it's best for you to return home and get a new visa there."

I tried to tell her that I couldn't do that, that I was on a very tight schedule and that at the end of the schedule and the convoluted paperwork trail a little girl waited for me, but she was already busy with another customer.

"Please," I said, "let me speak to your supervisor."

She frowned again, and called over the woman she'd spoken to earlier.

"Can I please speak to you about this problem?" I asked.

"There's nothing we can do," she said, "you must have a valid visa in order to receive a boarding pass to Hanoi."

"But can't you see they've made a simple mistake?" I said. I pointed to the dates and explained to her carefully that the Vice-Ambassador must have inverted the two dates. She shook her head.

"Perhaps that is what happened," she granted me, "but how do I know that? Perhaps the visa is actually expired. Perhaps they really don't want you to come to Hanoi."

"Why would you say that?" I asked.

"Because we have many problems with these visas issued in the United States for Vietnam."

I told her a very brief story of Hanh, how she was waiting, and how it all depended upon me leaving for Hanoi this afternoon in less than fifteen minutes. Surely this woman could help me.

"There's nothing I can do," she said, "but you can speak to the Vietnamese representative for the airline."

I sighed some relief. I thought someone with authority from the Vietnamese side surely could help.

"Yes," I said. "Please let me speak to him."

"He's not here now," she said, "but here is his cell phone number, you can call him. I think he should be on his way to the airport now."

5

I made my way through the crowd to a kind of telephone I'd never seen before. The instructions explaining how to use the phone were in Chinese and an English that made absolutely no sense to me. I looked frantically around for help but realized it was useless. There were odd slots for coins that I did not have and additional slots for special phone cards. There wasn't time to investigate so I picked up the receiver and dialed the cell phone number. I was shocked to hear what sounded like a connection being made; then a busy signal.

I dialed again and again and each time heard a series of odd clicks followed by the irritating international busy signal I'd heard so often over the years when I'd tried to call Hanoi from the U.S. I wasn't sure if the number was in fact busy or if I was dialing the phone incorrectly. I looked around again for help and dialed once more, expecting nothing more than the same noisy nonconnection, when suddenly a man answered.

He listened to a quick explanation of my problem. I wanted to believe that he sounded sympathetic. He told me that he was actually in the airport and that he'd be at the desk in a few minutes. I relayed this to the supervisor who only shook her head and turned away.

I had sweat through my shirt, and my kidneys, which I'd had problems with in the months preceding my trip, were beginning to ache and I worried that I'd get dehydrated and have more problems, even another stone. I tried to control my breathing, to calm myself and to think my way through the problem that threatened to swallow me whole.

6

The sight of the sweet, open face of the Air Vietnam representative from Hanoi making his way through the crowd pulled me out of that vortex of trouble. He came right to my side and introduced himself as Mr. Nguyen Thanh Nam, Airport Manager for Air Vietnam in Hong Kong, then asked to see my visa and ticket.

"This is very difficult," he said. "This visa has already expired, can't you see the date here?" He pointed and held the open passport close to my face.

"Yes, I can see it, but can't you also see that they've clearly made a mistake, that the dates for issue and expiration have been accidentally reversed?"

He laughed in a way that is often misunderstood by the American tourists who have begun to breeze in and out of Vietnam since Clinton lifted the embargo, but I understood well from my time in Vietnam: not a cruel laugh, but a laugh of acceptance of the enormity of consequences over which we have no control. The Vietnamese, with their long history of brutal invasion and hostile occupation by the Chinese, Japanese, French and Americans, know this enormity more fully than anyone with whom I've ever spent any intimate time. It is a laughter so deeply rooted in the culture that it's as much a part of growing up Vietnamese as ancestor worship.

"Yes," he said, "they have made a mistake, but I'm sorry to say it's only your mistake now. It will probably never be their mistake."

"There must be something you can do," I said. I was almost begging now and knew that soon I *would* beg, without hesitation.

"I'm sorry, there's nothing. You must return home and get another visa."

I could tell that he knew this request was unreasonable, but I could also tell that he had quickly calculated the chances that my situation was on the level, that the Vice-Ambassador really had made an error, and whether he could risk his job by giving me a boarding pass because all would be straightened out in Hanoi. I could tell by the look in his eyes that the calculations had added up on the side of discretion. He seemed as though he wouldn't budge.

I asked him if he'd sit down with me for a minute to talk. "In ten minutes the flight will leave," I said. "Just give me five minutes."

He agreed and we walked over to a nearby wall and sat on the floor against it.

"I'm on my way to Hanoi," I said, "to pick up an eight-year-old girl whom I'm adopting with my wife and my fifteen-year-old son. She lives in a very poor orphanage in Binh Luc, Nam Ha province. She never knew her father, whom her mother never married, and her mother is just now dying from an unnamed illness. This girl's name is Nguyen Thi Hanh and already we love her very much and want very much to give her a life." I paused to give Mr. Nguyen time to think, then continued.

"I teach at a university in the United States and I've taken some time off from my job to come to Hanoi. I'm on a very tight schedule. They expect me in Hanoi this afternoon and then in Binh Luc tomorrow. Many details must be taken care of, many papers signed and stamped. You know how it is," I said. He nodded and smiled and listened for the rest.

"If I don't keep to my schedule, I won't be able to complete all of the necessary paperwork in order to leave Vietnam with Nguyen Thi Hanh as I'd planned. I'd have to leave without her."

I was almost sure he could see that this would be a terrible thing for her. "When she was four years old," I told him, "she was begging on the street for food for her and her crippled mother."

I paused, took in a long breath, and studied his face. An opening that hadn't been there before took the form of an almost imperceptible light in his eyes; at the same time, I saw a worried furrow appear on his brow.

"I have many friends in Hanoi," I continued, and asked where in Hanoi he had grown up. When I told him that I was familiar with his street and convinced him by naming some nearby street-side restaurants and coffee shops, I knew that he was pleased.

"I have many friends in Vietnam," I repeated. "Perhaps you know some of them." I began to recite the names of my writer friends from Hanoi, Hue and Ho Chi Minh City. I could tell he recognized almost everyone I mentioned and was impressed. He said he had grown up reading most of their work.

I told him about some of my work in Vietnam as a translator of Vietnamese poetry: that I had published a book of these translations in English, a book of poems written by soldiers from the North who had died in the American war. I told him that General Giap himself had read the book and was so happy to see the poems of his former soldiers printed for American readers that he had sent his personal emissary to my guest house on Nguyen Du with an enormous bouquet of flowers to thank me. The emissary had said that the General remembered meeting me on one of my earlier trips to Vietnam. I took out an envelope of photographs of Nguyen Thi Hanh at the orphanage, and of my own family back home, and one of me standing with General Giap and Le Lu and Pham Tien Duat, two very important writers from Hanoi.

The line to board the plane was beginning to file past a woman taking tickets.

Mr. Nguyen looked at the photographs again and asked almost casually, as if time meant nothing, about the people in them. It pleased him to see my family, and he said that adopting this child was a kind and generous thing to do. He said that if he gave me a boarding pass and there was any trouble in Hanoi, he would surely lose his job and then could not support his wife and child, as well as his mother and father.

I knew he wasn't exaggerating. I had heard these stories many times. He kept looking at the picture of Nguyen Thi Hanh at the orphanage. Then he looked into my face for a long minute, sighed deeply and said he'd have to call Hanoi first, a friend he knew who worked at Noi Ba Airport, and he began dialing the cell phone.

My heart sank. I knew something about how difficult it was to reach Vietnam by phone. I cursed my own stupidity for not having checked my visa more carefully before I'd departed. Although the visa had arrived the morning of my departure and there would have been no time to have had a second visa issued, perhaps the Vice-Ambassador could have called ahead to Hanoi or to Hong Kong to somehow straighten out the mess. But I had been rushed. When I had opened the FedEx envelope with my passport, I quickly turned to the inside page and saw the official People's Republic of Vietnam seal stamped inside with some almost illegible numbers and words. Stupidly I assumed all was in order. There was no one to blame but myself. I thought of Nguyen Thi Hanh, waiting for me. I could not imagine a form of forgiveness that would ease this terrible mistake.

Miraculously, Mr. Nguyen reached someone after only a few seconds. I tried to translate and thought I heard him ask for the captain of airport security.

After a few more agonizing seconds he said, "Yes, Yes," a few times in Vietnamese, "Vung, Vung." He looked at the gate and clicked the cell phone shut.

He stared at the pictures once more, then quickly wrote down the name of a man I should ask for upon my arrival in Hanoi. He handed me a boarding pass. I shook his hand and tried to offer him money.

"I don't want that," he said. "I'm not doing this for money. I'm doing this for you and for Nguyen Thi Hanh."

I asked if he could fax a message ahead to a friend in Hanoi and he agreed. After I'd written the name, number and a brief message on a piece of scrap paper and handed it to him, I shook his hand, half embraced him, and walked to the gate. I handed my boarding pass to the woman at the gate and was ushered aboard the plane to take my place in the only empty seat.

7

I could hardly believe I was sitting there, strapped into the seat inside the cool atmosphere of the 727. I knew that once I got to Noi Ba Airport outside Hanoi my friends would be able to solve the visa problem.

Immediately after takeoff I released my seat belt, lowered my seat back and stretched out. I hadn't slept for two days and the hours I'd spent at the airport had drained me of the last of my energy. But I was smiling to myself too. I closed my eyes and thought about Nguyen Thi Hanh. I imagined what it would be like to see her tomorrow for the first time.

I fell asleep within the comfort of those thoughts and didn't move again until I felt a sudden jar; I thought at first we'd hit turbulence, then realized the short flight was over. We had landed at Noi Ba. I was back in my second home, the home of my heart. I looked out the small window across the tarmac and was surprised by how much the airport had grown since my last trip.

The Circle of Hanh

I thought too about that first return trip in 1986. I'd gone back with two other American writers as the guests of a retired North Vietnamese Army general named Kinh Chi. We were among the first American veterans to visit the North after the war. The American and Allied embargo was still in place and the Vietnamese, especially those in the North, were clearly still suffering from an all-consuming poverty and other lingering effects of our long war. The embargo had also made it difficult for us to travel from the U.S. to Vietnam, and the last leg of that trip, from Vientiane, Laos, to Hanoi, had put us in a very small, outdated prop-driven plane that resembled a Piper Cub painted military green, with "Air Lao" lettering painted in red on the small tail. The first few rows of seats were roped off, and piled high on the seats were boxes of live chickens and ducks. In the heat the stench was overwhelming. Our pilot, who looked to me to be about fifteen or sixteen, greeted us warmly just before takeoff. In remarkably clear English he told us not to worry about the plane. He said that it was old but he knew it well and could land it anywhere if he had to. He said that only last week he had landed it on Highway One near Hue. He said this to comfort us, I'm sure, but I remember feeling a moment of panic and almost deciding to get off the plane to try for some other kind of connection.

He smiled broadly to us, the three Americans and four or five Vietnamese, then he waved in a way that reminded me of Nixon's wave as he boarded the helicopter that would carry him away from Washington and the shame of his forced resignation.

As the Air Lao pilot climbed in the cockpit he put on a vintage World War II pilot's hat that was too big and fell over his ears. I worried that he wouldn't be able to see beyond the visor that must have also hung low over his forehead.

I could see into the cockpit. Either there wasn't a door, or he didn't bother closing it. There also didn't appear to be a copilot and I wondered if I could fly the plane if I had to. I watched him flip a few switches and wave to someone outside. I looked out and saw a small boy standing near the propeller. The boy grabbed the highest blade he could reach, stretched his small body until he stood on his toes and, with all the force he could muster, pulled down on the prop. An enormous cloud of white smoke exploded out of the engine, which sputtered, then roared, then sputtered again before it died. The pilot turned in his seat, waved to us again and gave us the thumbs-up before motioning once more to the boy outside, who once again used his whole body to crank the propeller down.

Again the air around the engine filled with white smoke. Again the engine sputtered, roared, sputtered a few more times, bit then caught hold and thundered in a way that made me think of the cars we drove as teenage boys in Lorain whose mufflers we had punched with holes to make them rumble like hot rods.

We taxied slowly to the end of the runway of hard-caked dirt that looked far too short to me, even for our small plane. At the end of the runway a small rise in the landscape loomed with tropical trees. Our boy-pilot gunned the engine hard until I thought that it would surely explode or the prop would fly off. Then I felt him let go of the brakes and we began to move at such a slow speed I was convinced we would never make it up; I reasoned that he was probably just taking a practice run to warm up the engine. But as we picked up a little more speed and got nearer and nearer the end of the short runway, it became clear to me that he was going for it.

I wanted to close my eyes but was too afraid. My shirt was wet with sweat in the Vientiane heat and my head spun with nausea brought on by my fellow fowl passengers and the heavy smell of fuel. At the last possible moment I watched the pilot pull back hard on the wheel and felt the plane lift, more suddenly than I had imagined possible, into a climb so steep we were all jarred back in our seats.

The chickens and ducks squawked wildly. I heard a strange noise that I first imagined was part of the plane tearing loose but realized was the underbelly of our plane scraping the tops of the banana trees at the end of the runway.

But we were airborne, and after climbing at that steep angle for a few minutes, the pilot leveled off the plane at what looked to me to be only about a thousand feet or so—which turned out to be our cruising altitude all the way to Hanoi. I could hear the ancient engine missing from time to time, not hitting on all of its cylinders but running nevertheless. The pilot turned around once more to smile and give us his thumbs-up, a gesture we all returned with gratitude.

I settled back in my small seat with a sense of accomplishment and great faith in our pilot, whom I believed probably could land his plane anywhere, as he'd told us before takeoff. I just hoped it would be at the airport in Hanoi.

Except for a few brief and terrifyingly inexplicable free falls through otherwise smooth air, the flight to Hanoi was short and uneventful. When we crossed the mountains of the central highlands where I had spent most of my time during the war, I began to see the Vietnam that I had remembered: the lush, emerald green that I could easily conjure behind my closed eyes.

Within an hour we banked sharply and began to circle in preparation for landing. In 1986 the Noi Ba Airport was hardly recognizable as an airport at all, and as we came in low over some small ridges, only a small tower became visible. The landscape surrounding the airport and the fields just beyond its single runway were still pockmarked with bomb craters that looked huge even from the air. I wondered why there were so many craters so long after the war. A few days later I would learn that filling in the craters was an almost impossible excavation project, especially since most of the work had to be done manually. Still burdened by the embargo, without much capital for anything other than the most rudimentary equipment and medical supplies, the Vietnamese were ill-prepared to do the job.

It was a complicated problem, General Kinh Chi would tell me a few days later. The rice fields were decimated by thousands of holes, some of them hundreds of feet in depth and width. Before the rice crop, Vietnam's only source of income at the time, could be planted and cultivated, the holes had to be filled and the fields leveled, work done mostly by hand and with the help of water buffalo. To fill one crater sometimes took months, and it would be years before the landscape would look as it had before the bombing.

During our month long stay in Vietnam on that first trip back, the General gradually became like a father to us all. He had fought against the French and then the Americans and he was highly regarded for his long service to his country. He was perhaps best known for having escorted the French general who had surrendered at Dien Bien Phu through the jungles and back to Hanoi. The North Vietnamese soldiers had nearly run out of food and medical supplies during the long siege. We learned from another retired officer that Kinh Chi, who was solely responsible for getting the French general to Hanoi in good health, had given his enemy what little food he had left. When the French general became ill with dysentery, Kinh Chi had given him his medicine.

Eventually Kinh Chi would come to hold our hands as we walked through Hanoi, the way men do in countries that don't demand a constant show of manliness. When we left he kissed our cheeks and cried openly. But during our first three or four days together he was stern, lecturing us in the grim offices of the War Crimes Commission in Hanoi on a sweeping and exhaustive range of subjects, including a detailed history of Vietnam beginning in the twelfth century, an explanation of the complexities of collectivization, the condition of the agricultural reform movement, and a long list of the terrible statistics: the dead and the maimed and the homeless.

It took more than a few days for us to realize that we were being "reeducated" by the General. We were the Commission's first American visitors and they didn't know what else to do with us. Kinh Chi finally wore us down with meetings and lectures that would sometimes last six or seven hours at one sitting, to the point where we had to say Enough. We wanted to get out and walk around the city and talk with the people.

Through Kinh Chi's generosity and kindness, and because he was so highly regarded, we were able to meet important people in the arts and in the government. We visited Bach Mai Hospital, and Ho Chi Minh's mausoleum and his wartime home. We went to orphanages and spent time with several committees that were part of the convoluted Marxist/Leninist system: the American Hanoi Friendship Committee, the Hanoi Writers' Union, the Central Committee for Vietnamese Culture, Literature and the Arts. We went to the Institute of Foreign Affairs. We danced with children at the Children's Palace, a school of the arts, and we ate lunch with workers at a factory that employed only those who had been severely handicapped in the war. All of the factory's equipment had been designed to be operated by men and women with only one arm, or no arms and one leg, or no arms or legs.

8

After two weeks we flew south with General Kinh Chi to Ho Chi Minh City, where for another two weeks we visited the southern half of the new regime and took day trips to other provinces and cities. The General was always at our side, teaching us almost image by image, face by face, a side of the war that none of us could ever have imagined possible.

Towards the end of that trip, I met a close friend of the General named Miss Tao in Ho Chi Minh City and everything changed for me. I didn't know for a long time what the consequences of that change would be, but I knew I would be a different kind of man from then on. One result of my meeting Miss Tao would be my decision to return to Vietnam to try to give back something of what I had helped take away. Another consequence would be my trip to pick up our eight-year-old daughter and bring her into our home so she might have a life of choices.

I'd gone back to Vietnam that first time with myself at the center of my thinking. Gradually, as I met people who had been my invisible enemy sixteen years before, that self began to lose its importance. In the face of the enormous struggle these people had endured for most of their lives, my brief involvement in the war and my imagined sacrifices seemed less and less important. I felt I was on the verge of some important understanding. Miss Tao pushed me over the edge.

9

The mock-up tiger cage at the War Crimes Museum in Ho Chi Minh City was too real, even for Miss Tao, who is stronger than most of us. The cage was six feet tall by four feet wide. A concrete platform twelve inches off the floor passed for a bed. Fastened to the foot of this so-called bed were iron shackles. Like the real tiger cages in which Miss Tao had spent more than a year, the top of the cell represented the actual "cage" portion of the prison. Four or five inches apart, the bars offered no protection: when it rained, it rained into the cell. During the hottest months, many prisoners were crammed into one cell to make the heat even more unbearable. When the weather turned cool and wet, people were left only one or two to a cage to prevent the possibility of body heat for warmth. There were no toilets, only two buckets, seldom emptied.

Miss Tao told me that she was fed twice a day during that year of imprisonment by our puppet regime. Most often, she said, she was given a small bowl of hard rice and a small portion of spoiled fish or meat that of course made her sick and eventually did irreparable harm to her liver and kidneys.

Miss Tao told me that during her imprisonment she would sometimes try to convert her guards to the way of what she called "the new Vietnam." Some of the guards responded by beating her. Some tortured her. Some dumped quicklime on top of her through the bars, blinding her temporarily, making it impossible for her to breathe. She continued her quiet and insistent appeals, pleading not for herself but for the people of Vietnam. She told me that she did it also to keep from going mad, to keep herself alive for as long as she could, although she was convinced that she, like so many others who had come there, would die.

During her student days at the Madame Curie School in Saigon, Miss Tao had joined the growing student opposition to the American war, marching in the streets and, towards the end of the war, collaborating directly with the North Vietnamese Army. Turned in by a neighbor, she was arrested when she was eighteen. She spent a full year in the tiger cage and two more years in a brutal prison on Puolo Condo Island. When she was released from prison she was partially paralyzed and severely malnourished, and had suffered serious damage to her central nervous system. She couldn't walk for a long time but managed after several months to get up onto crutches and become active once again in the antiwar movement. When Vietnam was liberated in 1975 she was recognized for her courage by the new regime, who took responsibility for her care. She had recovered enough by the time I met her in 1986 to assume a position with the War Crimes Museum but some days she was still too weak to get out of bed.

We sat in the mock-up tiger cage and talked. She was sweet and shy and pronounced her English sentences slowly and carefully. She was still able to smile and even laugh out loud but there was a great sadness in her eyes that I could not turn away from. I could hardly keep my heart from beating wildly away. Her lips quivered as she told me of her imprisonment and the nightmares that she recounted now, after so many years, with the strange satisfaction that comes to those who have practiced the words over and over.

In one dream, she says, she is dragged from her sleep through the streets of her neighborhood in Saigon. This makes her feel ashamed, she says. Vaguely familiar faces line the street and laugh at her predicament. People point at her. She is dragged to a cell where she faints and awakes sweating and crying out. No one answers, she says. She is at the bottom of a very deep and dark hole. When she looks up towards a pin of light coming in from the top, she can barely make out the faces of her mother and her sister. Their lips move, she tells me, as though they spoke to her, but no sound comes down into the hole. In the dream she pleads with them for help and they plead back soundlessly until her own screaming wakes her.

10

Later we sit down together in the museum office to listen to our friend Kinh Chi talk. Miss Tao has on a lovely *ao dai,* the long silk dress worn by the women of Vietnam, especially in the South. The *ao dai* is hand-embroidered with many small white roses and delicate leaves. I watch her finger the flowers, stretching the silk to make the flowers come alive, as if she were seeing them for the first time. She fingers the flowers and sips her tea so carefully that I can't help but stare at her. She watches the trees that surround the building we're in, light streaking through their branches as if through bars. She tilts her head and watches the trees as if only this moment she had opened her eyes after many years of darkness.

After a while I see her suddenly hold her face in her hands. After the tea and sweet tangerines, after the last light has drifted away from us, she drifts away too. She travels to a place I can never know: a black and empty hole where men did to her as they pleased because she loved her country. This drifting seems the only indulgence she allows herself, but it surprises me because it is so real, so visible.

I imagine that she has no choice in this journeying. I imagine that her way of staying on the earth is to keep one part of herself back there in the tiger cage. The horror of that year must have taken so much of her that she needs to go back there in her mind to stay whole.

Suddenly she shakes her head as if waking from a deep sleep, her brain still tangled in dream. She reaches for the tea, which has turned cold. Although she doesn't know it, Miss Tao is what I left behind those sixteen years before. During that first trip back to Vietnam I'd caught glimpses of the boy I had been in the war: here and there a fleeting shadow would pass. After being with Miss Tao that day I knew that Vietnam would never be the same for me again. The old proud songs were gone now: the songs of napalm and mines, the songs of burning shit and pulling guard, the songs of the surrounding blues. The old songs wouldn't work anymore and the boy that I had been back there, the boy I'd been reaching back to all these years, was gone too. Not lost exactly, but drifting in a green, misty place that is neither his world nor anyone else's.

The Circle of Hanh

I had been haunted for a long time, exiled from my body and from the world itself, looking for a home that could sustain what I had become. Miss Tao helped me find that home, that country that is my heart split in two, and Miss Tao is why I'm sitting in the cool 727 on the tarmac of the Noi Ba Airport, 1996, coming to get my daughter, coming back to try to make the circle whole again.

Part Two

Stories from
the Hidden Book

II

The circle made whole is a story, but to make the circle whole, I have to go back. I have to fill in the blanks of memory.

When that man in An Khe threw me a copy of *Crime and Punishment,* I had never read a book straight through in my life. My family kept an ill-read bible somewhere in the house. Once or twice that I can remember, I picked it up as a child still too young for catechism or for church and asked my mother or father what it was.

"That's a book about God," my father would say. "That's a good book to read."

But he never read to me from it. He was tired from his long hours in the mill. He never said much more about the book than that, even after I'd ask him things like, Who wrote it? Or, How could someone write a book about God? Or, Did they see God? Did they talk to God?

Years later I would pick up that Bible again and find, in the back, on two or three sheets of tissue-thin end pages, in already-fading pencil, a treelike shape. Written across the unruled, awkward branches were the names of my people on my mother's and my father's sides, going back as far as whoever wrote them down could remember. When I found those names scrawled across the branches of the tree I thought I understood some things: why they'd kept the Bible even though they never read it, and how they wanted somehow to attach the history of our people, bloody as it turns out to be, to the pure word of Scripture and thus somehow save us from ourselves and our history.

12

I also found a thick paperback hidden away in my mother's dresser during one of those frantic, mindlessly driven searches children conduct when they're left alone in the house.

The writer's name didn't mean anything to me, and the title made me think it was only one of those stupid books about love like I'd seen one of my cousin's girlfriends read; on the cover was a not-quite-realistic painting of a long-haired woman bent backwards, held by a man who looked as though he had makeup on. His hair was slicked back and shining.

The woman was leaning back that way in his arms so you could see just enough of her breasts to make you want to pick the book up. I did pick up books like that now and then, but after a sentence or two I realized the words had nothing to do with those breasts nearly falling out of her dress.

I wondered why this book was hidden away in my mother's dresser. I wondered why, if they had only one book besides a bible that no one read, it was this book, and so I started to read it. I must have been thirteen or fourteen when I found the book. It stayed in my mother's dresser for years, among her garters and stockings, and whenever I had the chance, I'd read from it. My time was always short (I read slowly then, as I do now, moving my lips. Still I like to feel the words on my tongue, rolling off my lips), since I never knew when someone would come home. I didn't want my mother or father to catch me with the book even though I hadn't yet figured out why I shouldn't be reading it.

I'd read a few pages at a time, looking for whatever it was that made them buy this book and hide it in their bedroom. For a long time I didn't find anything. I didn't understand what was happening in the story. The people in the story had lives that were very different from mine. Although the book evoked a world that seemed to exist beyond the pages, I wondered if these lives were real, and that made me wonder if my life was real.

I think now that the power of the word had begun to take root inside of me. Sometimes when I read from the book there was a fleeting blaze of an unnameable knowing that streaked through my brain and then, just as quickly, was gone. There was a vague and terrifying sense that I was somehow a part of the story; that I was connected to the people in the story; that we were all connected. I think now that must have been the word doing its work on me.

Still, more than once I gave up on that book. Months would go by without my even thinking of it. The reading was hard and mostly unrewarding, given my urgent and fundamental adolescent needs. I wanted to find the dirty parts I knew had to be there somewhere, but there was so much talk about nothing that I almost gave up on it entirely, until one sun-streaked empty Saturday afternoon when I found myself home alone and wondering.

I was thinking about a girl named Sally whom I'd spent a lot of time with back then. We were doing what we thought people in love were supposed to do because we thought we were in love.

We were going steady, which meant in those days that I'd bought her a cheap man's ring at Woolworth's. She wore it on a chain around her neck to show everyone that she was mine.

Sally was a cheerleader, and on Friday afternoons, after school and before the game, I walked her home. Her mother and father were at work, and her sister left us alone. I was an unconsciously dangerous boy of sixteen by then, and we would make out in the basement rec room.

I was a lucky boy too, because she'd have on her cheerleading clothes. She wore a wool pleated skirt cut well above her knees, black panties that felt like silk, and a vest cut short so you could see her navel when she jumped up to cheer, or when she stretched out on the Naugahyde couch, where we would gradually tangle ourselves up with each other, kissing so long and so hard and sucking on each other's tongues so fiercely I thought sometimes I would die from it.

She made me feel as if I could take on anything. She let me lift that pleated cheerleading skirt up and press myself against those black panties. Each time we learned a little more, and eventually she figured out how to wrap her legs around me with that skirt hiked up so I could feel her sex against mine. We sucked each other's tongues and humped that way for hours. Sometimes I'd even come in my pants, and afterwards I'd have to hold my hands in front of my crotch in what must have been a painfully obvious and futile attempt to hide the stain.

I learned to stop in the upstairs bathroom on my way down to the rec room; with an enormous wad of toilet paper, I'd make a kind of sanitary napkin that I shoved in my underwear to soak up the come. When I was on her that way, swirling in that drunken, inexplicable pleasure, I'd think about Sharon too, another cheerleader from another life, who as my teenage baby-sitter had done some nasty business on me when I was four or five. Carefully and with what must have been an exquisitely practiced grace, Sharon had drawn me into the wildly confused and imaginative pathology that she had shaped into a game she called wrestling.

We played our game only after my sister had gone to bed and Sharon knew for sure that my mother and father would be out late. I knew it was wrong but didn't know why. What came to frighten me most was that I began to long for our time together, though I didn't have a word for longing then. I knew somehow that we were moving closer and closer to trouble. I knew too that I would follow Sharon into that trouble, no matter what, because whatever it was she made happen in me would be worth the trouble.

Dry-humping that way so hard and so long with Sally, I'd sometimes rub myself raw. When I got deep into those places that you may find only at the threshold of the final passage, Sally and Sharon would begin to come together in my mind; they became one person, and I liked it that way.

13

It was November in Lorain, Ohio, just enough cold air off the lake to make you feel a little more alive. I was thinking about Sally, from the day before, and about Sharon because somewhere inside me I almost always thought of her.

I hadn't seen Sharon for more than ten years but she had become part of me in ways that I did not understand, except through the tangled nerves at the center of an almost-lost memory.

I must have touched myself that afternoon too, which made me go back to my mother's dresser and take out the book. I took it out from under her lingerie and opened it somewhere in the middle and tried again to find the mystery.

I didn't know what I'd really found that afternoon until a long time afterwards; not until one drugged and drunken postwar night when a woman I'd met in a bar, and with whom I'd wandered into a part of Boston I'd never seen before, suddenly pushed me onto my back into a weedy city garden where we'd stopped to kiss and grope each other in our loneliness, in the midnight rain. She raised her dress and took me inside her. We rolled around in the muddy garden. She tore my shirt open and rubbed the mud all over me and then she fucked me so hard I felt my body rise into the rain-hammered night sky.

But this November Saturday, many years before the postwar drunken fucking in the muddy garden, I learned why my mother and father had hidden the book.

I found a place in the story where a man and a woman were naked in the mud. He was inside of her. They both said the word *Fuck*. They said it in a way I'd never heard before. They said it without anger and somehow lovingly, I thought. They both said *Fuck* over and over and they played with how they said it and made it sound sweet on the page.

The woman picked flowers and braided them into the man's pubic hair and he did the same to her. What struck me most was that they were naked outside in the mud. I could not fathom why they would want to do those things in the mud, or why the man talked to the woman so strangely in a language that I knew was my language but was somehow different too: the Fuck word said alongside the thees and thous.

I read those few pages over and over that Saturday afternoon. I thought about being with Sally the day before in her cheerleader's dress, and how she liked to wear a flower in her hair on those days. I thought about Sharon too, how she got on top of me when I was four years old in my Lone Ranger pajamas and rocked herself into bliss, with my legs stiffening and terrifyingly wonderful things happening inside my body that I hadn't known until then and didn't understand enough to fear.

I took the book into the bathroom and read the passage again about the braiding of flowers into the tangled, wet pubic hair of the man and the woman. I heard the man and the woman say the word *Fuck,* and I masturbated. I got dizzy and almost didn't hear the front door open. My mother called across the house and I shouted that I was in the john. I got the book back where it belonged and for a long time I believed that my mother had no idea that I'd been reading it, or using it that way. Of course they must have known after a while because I almost wore that book out, or at least those three or four pages anyway. I stained the cover with soap dirty from my hands. Like the penciled names in the Bible's tissue-thin endpapers, some words were already disappearing from the pages.

14

That book about Lady Chatterley and her gamekeeper was my first book, and though I must have read only a dozen pages or so, I read them many times. Without knowing what I was doing, I had let the sweet human music of the story take hold inside me, where it simmered, where it felt like it belonged.

Even after I started bringing books home from school, it never occurred to me that they were things I actually had to hold in my hands for very long. It didn't occur to me that I had to read a whole book. I'd never seen anyone read a book in my house, or in the houses of my grandparents. Books were what they gave you at school for homework.

My father agreed, I know, and although my mother seemed to see more importance, maybe even more possibility, among books, she also saw dangers there. Reading some things in books could hurt you. The knowing could be dangerous because there were some questions you were not supposed to ask; things that were better left unknown, or unsaid.

Without my mother or father actually ever saying it this way, I grew up believing that books were useless because they were only words, and words didn't get work done. Words didn't put food on the table or clothes on your back. My people believed that reading history was a waste of time because we could not change what had already happened, and that what you learned in English class was a way of talking that you would never use, and that science was a world where God didn't exist, a world that said we came from monkeys.

"Do I look like I came from a monkey?" my father said when I asked him.

That was the long and the short of it. There was never anything said in my house about how books could change your life, and if there had been, people would have laughed, or worse.

15

Instead of books and, for a long time, instead of television, we had stories. I don't believe we understood then that our stories were the same as books. Back then it would not have occurred to me to write those stories down, but the richness of story was a living, palpable thing in my family; the taste of the well-told story on your lips was like a kiss, and the light in the eyes of the others like a gift or a promise.

To tell a story well was a prized accomplishment that took years to master among my people and we practiced chiefly around the coal stove in the quiet evenings after work.

One of my father's favorite stories to tell, even to strangers and always much to my shame because he told it with an odd relish for its grim details, had to do with an accident I had when I was three years old. We were living in an upstairs apartment. The apartment was in a dangerous state of ruin, and my mother warned me about where I could wander and what parts I had to stay away from.

As my father told it, I was a slow walker and at three I still preferred to crawl. I hugged the floor like a dizzy man hugs the ground after spinning too long in a dance, he'd say.

My mother was in the kitchen, getting supper ready for my father before he came home from the mill. He worked hard and was always so hungry that, fascinated, I would watch him hard and closely for the first five or ten minutes of the meal. He ate with seriousness and such concentrated effort that it seemd the rest of us weren't there, that this meal might be his very last.

My mother was probably occupied with supper and with caring for my sister. I have a vague memory of the black telephone ringing and ringing and my mother not answering, and a memory too of something boiling over on the stove so that the gas flames flared up blue and yellow.

During this confusion in the kitchen I must have crawled out on the ruined landing. I don't remember why I was on the landing. I knew it was forbidden territory. It was rotten and shaky and led to a steep set of equally rotten and shaky stairs that led to the street.

I don't even remember my fall.

I must have made my way out of the small kitchen, out across the landing and somehow to the top of the stairs, without my mother seeing me. I could still hear the phone ringing in the kitchen. I could smell the spilled grease burning on the gas stove.

I don't remember the fall itself, but rather only the hanging on as I fell: desperate, useless attempts to grab on to the stairs to keep myself from falling farther, my fingernails searing and tearing and burning as I tried to hang on to the rotting wood that filled my fingers with splinters. Suddenly I found myself at the bottom of the stairs, remarkably standing upright.

I must have paused there for a moment, nurtured deeply beyond my pain in the shock and wonder of standing for the first time as if to walk. A great quiet filled the stairwell and the rest of the apartment, and for a moment I must have thought that no one had heard me fall. I hadn't called out to anyone. I was so frantically and hopelessly trying to stop my fall that there wasn't time to call out. There was only a long, drawn-out moment of silence of a kind I'd never known before, inside of which I was being changed.

I heard a downstairs door suddenly flung open and I saw the huge form of our downstairs neighbor lady standing before me. Although her door must have been only five or six feet from where I'd landed at the bottom of the stairs, by the time she reached me she was already out of breath. She was heaving, in fact, her face flushed and her eyes wide in what I know now was terror. She looked at me standing there for a second or two. Then she looked down at my fingers and she began to scream.

Her scream seemed to take on its own life. It grew in strength and volume as it spread from the bottom of the landing, out the door, up the stairs and to my mother's ears in the kitchen. It was a scream so painfully real and deep and sad and frightened that I could barely imagine that it came from a human being. It seemed more like the screams I'd heard animals make: rabbits or pigeons or spring lambs my grandfather raised and slaughtered for food in his backyard while I sat nearby, watching.

16

First I heard and then I saw my mother race and almost fall, herself, down those steep, rotting stairs. When she came to my side
and stood next to the neighbor woman, who was still screaming,
she too looked down at my fingers and began to scream, and their
screams became a chorus.

I looked down at my bloody fingers: shards of wood were
sticking up and out from under three or four fingernails of each
hand where the wood had embedded itself deeply into the skin
below the nails.

But I did not add to the screaming. I think I began to sob a little,
but I don't remember the pain. I think I sobbed for the trouble I
knew I was causing other people, and the trouble I would cause
myself too for being out on the landing where I knew I wasn't
supposed to be. I stared down at my bloody fingers and then I
walked out on a small porch above the weedy backyard. I have no
earthly idea where I might have been going, but I remember that
I was walking, on my own, and not crawling, and that brave thing
is what sustained me.

17

When my father told this story, he liked to say that this was the moment he'd come home from work. He would say he'd just gotten off the bus on the corner by Bonk's Bar and had walked half of the block to our apartment when he heard the screams and knew there was trouble. He began to run, and when he got to the porch he saw me with my bloody fingers held before me like a man in a dream, walking towards the last set of steps that would take me down to the street. He would laugh a low chuckle whenever he told this part and then he'd pause for a long time.

We didn't read books in our house so I don't know where he learned to tell it that way. I don't know how he learned the pacing that keeps you waiting for the next word, and the next, as if your life depended on hearing all of it, word by careful word leading to an inevitability that would give you some release.

After that deep laugh and the pause that he'd let linger until he knew he had to go on, he'd say that truly, the first thing that came to him when he saw me there on the porch, sobbing, with my bloody fingers held out before me, the hallway still mad with the loud screams of my mother and our neighbor, was that I was walking and not crawling. That made him smile, but in his telling he was quick to add that he never stopped moving towards me. He called to my mother for a rag and wrapped my hands in it and lifted me in his arms and began to run towards the nearby house of a neighborhood doctor of dubious credentials.

Things get blurry. In his muscled arms, with the screams of my mother and of our neighbor beginning to fade as we moved away from the apartment, I felt as if we were crossing into another way of being.

18

I don't remember the falling, but the hanging on as I fell, and I remember the doctor, a heavy-bodied man who spoke with a thick accent and always wore the same soup- and bloodstained white coat. I remember the two nurses and my father holding me down as the doctor pulled out the splinters. And I remember the pain that came upon me then.

The word, no matter how well said, can never be the thing, although sometimes when we work hard and we're lucky, we may come close. Yet I would only risk diminishing the clear, intense and singular nature of that pain if I tried to tell it here. I would only diminish how beautiful the pain was in its clarity and how it seemed to connect my body in a way I'd never felt connected before.

It must have been the nerve endings in my fingers, my neurologist friend says. He says that some of the splinters probably embedded themselves directly into the nerves, so that when the splinters were touched or moved in any way, a network of pain signals was sent twisting through my body, connecting all of those receptors at once.

The word can never be the thing, but I was only three years old and it took two nurses and my six-foot-three-inch millworker father to hold me down as the doctor pulled the splinters out.

When my father told this story, he'd say the doctor didn't believe in giving children shots for pain in those days. This unlikely but affordable doctor of ours, who also pulled teeth in emergencies, said that children didn't feel pain the same way and therefore didn't need the shot.

I imagine my screaming must have lasted until we were all pale and sobbing, until I was lifted, my fingers thick and heavy with huge wraps of bloodstained white gauze, until once again I was lifted into my father's arms where I felt safest and most loved and most cared for.

He carried me outside and lifted me into the backseat of my uncle's car; my mother must have called him when we were gone. He had waited outside in the street with her because she could not bear the sight of these things. My father lifted me into the backseat of my uncle's car, where my mother cradled my head in her lap. Almost immediately, sleep lulled me from the pain to the memory of pain.

I woke up as my uncle wheeled his oversized Buick into the weedy side yard of our apartment building. It was dark by then but a light shone from the top of the stairs I'd fallen down, and I suddenly hated that place, and I feared those stairs.

That night, as my father lifted me from the backseat of my uncle's car, my fingers throbbing, the pain shooting up my wrists and arms, I blamed that apartment for all of my woes. I hated those stairs like you might hate a man, and as my father carried me up to the bedroom I shared with my sister, I was already plotting against them. I would pay them back somehow. I would smash them with my father's hammer, or burn them down. I swore to myself that I'd do whatever it took to make the stairs feel like my throbbing fingers felt, and like my empty heart felt, because I'd failed, because the stairs and my father were right: I was a baby. I had to crawl.

My father has always told that story best because my own remembering is so clouded with pain. I didn't know how to say the words or even think them then, but in the weeks and months to come, as I heard him tell it over and over—in spite of the fact that my pain and my failure to walk like a big boy sat at the story's real center—I loved how he shaped the story into a living thing.

When I'd hear him tell it, even years later, with his calculated timing and his precise evocation of detail, I could still feel my fingers as the doctor pulled those splinters out. How little I knew then about what was really happening to me: that the story's real importance had nothing to do with me, or with my falling, or with my fingernails filling with rotten splinters.

I think now that my father knew how our stories can save us, although he didn't learn it from books. He learned it from the telling and the retelling. He learned it because like the rest of us, he had no choice but to live as hard as he could inside the storm of his years, and because he understood that our chances to carve a small piece of our own telling out of the world's wall of loud talk are rare, and that no matter what the world has given you, you'd better take those chances when you can.

19

Remembering my father that way, seeing him tell his stories from all those years ago in my mind, I think about how different I am as a man with my own son because of how my father was with me. Because of those differences, I wonder what my son's life must feel like, what it must be like to be him.

My son is sixteen years old and he loves Shakespeare. He quotes from *Hamlet* and *Romeo and Juliet*. He has never been beaten with a belt. Like most sixteen-year-old boys he's sloppy about his room and he dodges homework and he would rather hang out with the dubious schemes teenage boys devise than read books. But he found his Shakespeare and likes it, so when he looks out on the world, he sees it from a very different place than I saw it from as a boy; he sees that the world is inhabited by soliloquy, and that means something.

One storm torn night after my son's girlfriend had called him long-distance to say that it was over between them, he called me out in the yard to show me the clouds, pushed wildly before a full moon by a high wind that shook the house.

He didn't want advice or consolation. He's far too smart to fall for an It-will-be-all-right speech from me. He knows already that it won't be all right, that in some ways it will never stop hurting.

He didn't want to talk. He wanted me to see the storm-torn night sky with him, that's all.

We watched it for a long time without speaking. I thought he was trying to find some kind of peace there, or some kind of order for his life that he imagined was falling to pieces because this first beautiful girl who had loved him would not love him again. Earlier that night he had sobbed deeply in his bed and said over and over to me, "It can't be real. It can't be really happening."

To suffer the attention and then the loss of beauty hurts no less at fifteen than it does at thirty or forty. I think in some ways it must hurt even more.

Without looking away from the sky that night, his face still tear-streaked and his eyes frozen in that rare empty-but-searching stare, he said, very quietly and with a lovely music to his voice, *I am at odds with fortune* and he meant it. He felt it and he understood that he could find peace in the words.

In this at least I find peace too, in the face of my sometimes dangerously clumsy, sometimes weak and selfish fathering. Knowing that he is blessed with words in this way, I am blessed too because I know that words can save you. I know that stories can allow escape from the terrible, trapped and lonely nights and can even lift your life away from a tangled jungle war.

Somehow my father and my people taught me what I have taught my son even though the place I saw the world from at sixteen was not inhabited by books, or by written words worked over and made right with care. Somehow, all of my people have been touched by the grace of stories, and we have all been saved by our stories in the face of hardship and loss and pain. I want to call those stories back now.

Part Three

Wrestling Sharon

20

To call the stories back I have to go to that childhood, because everything begins with Sharon, or with the story of Sharon, which stays alive and grows inside me even still. I want to tell you about my brief time with her, not for the pity of the story, or for the need to be forgiven. I was not a victim of anything except the spinning out of my own life. I was willing to follow Sharon into the reckless game she invented because I have always wanted to feel all of the world.

I want to tell you how our hours of wrestling helped shape me into who I am and how I love and how I am unable to love.

⌒

Whenever I came in from the leaf-choked backyard of the apartment we rented in the small house on 30th Street and smelled the undeniable scent of TV dinners in the oven, I knew my mother and father would be going out and that I would be wrestling Sharon.

Sometimes I like to think about it this way: my mother and father were in their twenties. They were what you'd call poor today, yet in the black-and-white photographs they've saved, they look to me like movie stars from the Forties, although I don't think they knew this, as theirs was a gracefully unconscious way of being.

They were twenty-three or -four, and they looked good, and it didn't take a lot of money then to drink beer around a loud juke-box in Lorain.

My handsome father sold stainless-steel pots and pans for a while, before he got on at the mill. He was tall and muscular, with thick black curly hair that I imagine must have gotten him in more than one lonely door. He sold pots and pans to brides he found in the newspaper's wedding announcements. To close the deal, he'd "do a dinner": fat-marbled roast beef, carrots, boiled and buttered potatoes, onions, green beans, salad, heavy gravy made from grease, and apple pie à la mode. I went with him a few times. I would help carry the pots and pans and the food into the house of the hostess, as he called the women, but I was not allowed to speak.

While he cooked I was to stand back and do what I was told. My father did all of the serving too, and during dinner I stood in the kitchen in a way that allowed me to see him at the table, eating with the bride and her guests and praising the virtues of stainless steel. I was to stand without being seen, and watch for signals he had taught me: the "more gravy" and "more water" signals, the "start the pie warming" signal.

Afterwards, he would clean the pots himself in a demonstration designed solely to show how easy the work would be, although even then I knew that lie; I had seen how he had practiced at home, and how much work it took to scrub the burnt pots clean with sharp cleansers. The labor was almost hidden by his smile and the easy way he had with strangers.

My mother stayed home with my sister and me those days, although she had worked long hours before this in a war factory in Lorain, and later, when my father labored in the mill beside the blast furnace's rumbled heat, my mother worked in the meat locker of the A&P. I have to turn away from the metaphors here. I have to hide my face from their shadows. I only want to see my parents as they were: so young and pretty, my father with a car and some dough in his pocket. It was 1956 and things were looking up, so Friday evenings sometimes they'd get dolled up, as my mother would say, after work, and she would put two TV dinners in the oven for my sister and me as we played in the backyard of that apartment house on 30th Street that we shared with a drunk who pissed on the heater in winter.

My sister and I played a game of rolling in the fallen leaves, huge piles of broad oak leaves heavy as flesh, thick all through the small backyard. Years later my sister told me that to hold off her own darkness then, she'd sometimes imagine that backyard and those leaves, the two of us swimming in them all over each other while our mother and father got dolled up in our small apartment lit with all the light they could burn. My sister said that when she thought of those times, a great peace would come into her.

After the sun had burned past our knowing, my mother would call us in, as the street lights were just working their way on, the cold coming in off the lake like a foreign thing. When I opened the back door, which led directly into the small kitchen, I would smell the TV dinners.

I only need to remember that smell to feel a twisting in my body; not like pain exactly, but more a contorted guilt, and an absence of some needful thing I couldn't name then. I'd get sick to my stomach; sometimes I'd vomit in secret; sometimes I'd swallow it down and go on because I had to eat. First I'd be sick, and then I'd acquiesce in a way I'd learned in order to survive, which is the acquiescence of the fearful.

When I smelled the TV dinners I'd think, *That's it,* and I would know that my fate was sealed irrevocably for the night, my mind and body not my own. TV dinners in the oven meant my mother and father were going out, and going out meant that Sharon would come to care for me and my sister, who was five.

I don't know where they found her, this Sharon, but I remember her clearly. I remember her face, and her black eyes always darting, always distracted, and her full hips, and her white bobby socks, and her high school cheerleading jacket, and her bag of tricks.

As my sister and I sat down to eat, my father would take the car to pick up Sharon. My sister and I would already be into our dinners. I would lick the juices from the foil top. The coal stove made the kitchen a toasty retreat from the cold evening's air, and we lingered there, in the way of children, as if our quiet talk and click of forks would never end.

We had just been called in from the leaves, where for a while we had become other children, lighter and more free, a feeling I've gone back to look for more than once but could not find, and we would wash our face and hands, put our shoes out on the back porch and sit down to our dinners.

Then my father and Sharon would come in. My mother would be standing in the kitchen trying to remember something, vaguely happy, it seems to me, beautiful in her going-out style, and sweet-smelling. I would have such longing for her, of a kind I still don't understand, that it was all I could do to stop myself from holding on to her. I couldn't tell her that I didn't want her to leave. I couldn't let her see that the thing that waited was already inside of me. So instead I watched Sharon's every practiced move when she came in, and I mopped up the last of the gravy with my bread.

21

I have a friend whom I love because he tells me the hard truth about myself: he says that I only tell what the others did to me, and never what I did to the others.

Okay. What I did to the others was to allow, and what I allowed Sharon, this girl whose era in my life is only a moment's dark rapture, was to lead me through a ritual that emerged and unfolded and revealed itself in almost imperceptible degrees, those random evenings my mother and father went out into their lives and their cool music.

My mother liked to kiss and hug good-bye then, but already I was drawing back from her. I would crouch by my bedroom window and watch my father waiting for her in his idling Chevy coupé, smoke from his Lucky Strike a lonely curlicue to nowhere, until my mother joined him, laughing. I would watch them pull away until the taillights vanished around the corner.

Soon afterwards, the order of all things would change. Sharon would call my sister and me into the small living room and turn the TV on. We watched a show in which different people came on to a stage: some sang; some danced in black shoes that made a slapping sound; some only stood on the stage and said things I didn't think were funny but that made other people laugh. Sharon laughed. I think she laughed too loudly. She said words I knew we weren't supposed to say. The way she watched the TV and laughed and swore scared me, so for as long as I could, I would stay close to my sister.

We watched what Sharon wanted until my sister and I began to drift off to sleep. I didn't know if my sister knew what Sharon and I did after she'd gone to sleep; sometimes I would watch her face to see. I imagined her in her room alone those nights. The apartment was small, the walls so thin you could almost always hear muffled voices. I wondered what she must have thought or felt when she heard us in the small living room, lying on a blanket before the television, doing the game Sharon called Wrestling.

Now I know that it changed my sister. Now I know that she huddled in bed those nights and choked her crying back.

But back then I had no choice but to believe that she didn't know, that no one knew. Alone sometimes I even hoped out loud to God that the "it" could be kept forever behind a shroud like a monster or a sickness, although even then I knew that God could not save me. I stayed close to my unsuspecting sister for as long as I could those nights. There was a quietude around her like a blanket; she was oblivious, it seemed, to me and my need for her to protect me.

I could never stay long enough. At ten or so Sharon would send us to wash and brush and put on our pajamas for bed. When I'd pass by Sharon standing in the doorway to my room, her hand on her hip, her bobby socks around her ankles, she would lean her whole self into me and I would smell a scent on her that I smelled nowhere else. It always made me think of fresh-mown grass just beginning to rot.

"Wear the Lone Ranger pajamas," she'd say, "the ones with flaps." She always said this same thing. She would lean towards me, and in her husky voice whisper, "I like those pajamas. Those are best for wrestling."

Then she'd laugh and slap me on the back and swing her hip to send me through the door. I did what I was told because there was no other imaginable way to live.

But Lord, there was something else there, a twist in the story, an unsayable incongruity I felt most powerfully in my stiffening legs; a deep but not abiding pleasure I came to long for, even need. I know it now as the kind of need that dooms us to haunt night streets if we have it too soon.

It is not easy to deliver myself back to those endlessly unfolding minutes. I have always kept a curtain there, heavy, like the cloth we use to wrap the dead. I don't know what it is I fear, except seeing the thing I was those nights with her, the thing I had to be.

I'd put on my Lone Ranger pajamas as I was told. They were my special pair, painted with silver bullets on a black belt, and silver guns, and the man himself in his mask, sitting high atop his rearing golden horse.

Those pajamas that Sharon liked best had a flap in the back too, so you could do your business at either end without taking them off.

I'd put on my Lone Ranger pajamas and for a few minutes I would stand before the spidered mirror and dip my mother's black comb in the thick green hair gel. I would stare hard into that boy's face but could never catch him unaware; always he seemed to look past me. I would follow his gaze out of the room and down the hall to Sharon's side, as if to say good night.

We'd say good night and march to bed as if to sleep because that was what was expected of us. That was what I had learned to do: march to bed in my Lone Ranger pajamas and lie there in the dark, waiting for her.

That room stays with me. The muted streetlight cutting through my bedroom window, the traffic noise, the voices rising from the street, some blood let there among the men and women in the summer's dark impatience. I waited for Sharon to come, fearing that she would, fearing more that she wouldn't.

22

One day in the summer of Sharon's second year with us, we moved suddenly from that apartment on 30th Street to an upstairs apartment on 17th Street next to St. Peter's Catholic Church, with its rock altar and outdoor holy pond, where my friends and I would play the growing-up games, and sin and confess our sins, and sin again.

My father showed up one early summer afternoon with somebody's beat-up pickup truck and started throwing our stuff, which my mother was frantically boxing, in the back of the truck, as if we were running away from something. It was strange to see him home in the middle of the day, and I wondered with a momentary sick fear if it had to do with Sharon and our wrestling.

I didn't know why we were leaving with our stuff, or where we were going. I didn't understand why my father was suddenly home from work in the middle of the day, or why my mother moved around our small apartment so frantically. She had abandoned her usual grace and care with our things as she stuffed them into boxes and bags. Before my father came home, I asked her twice why she was emptying the drawers and putting our things in boxes and where we were going. Twice she said, "Wait for your father, he's coming home. He'll be here soon."

After the truck was stacked high with the shabby interior of our lives, my father tied a tarpaulin across the back. He said "tarpaulin" when I asked what the thing was that he tied to the truck, and like some kind of stupid, useless anchor, I clung to that word the whole rest of the evening and night. I said it quietly to myself. I loved the way it felt in my mouth. Tar-pu-lin.

But no one said anything about Sharon. I was safe. During the rest of that afternoon my father made a few trips in the borrowed truck while my mother continued to pack. My sister and I were told to stay in the yard, and although we had played there almost every day and had invented endless games to pass our time, we didn't play then. We stood around the yard in wonder without speaking and without ever looking into each other's eyes.

Shortly after my father had left with the last truckload of our things, he got dropped off at home. We were waiting for him in the backyard with our last few things in a pile before us. My mother was quiet. Wind came up high in the oaks, turning the leaves over to their white sides. I looked through the yard towards the back porch. I felt a need to say good-bye.

"Why are we moving?" my sister whined.

"It's a better place," my mother said.

We wanted a better place.

My father shook hands with the man who dropped him off in the pickup truck. My father walked over to us without looking at anyone in particular. He studied the pile of our things, then said he'd make one more check. I said I'd go with him. He walked quickly through the empty apartment, where only our human smells remained. More than once I tried to linger there. I tried to gather something up in my brain but he said, "Let's go," and jerked me by the arm. He did it gently. He wanted to be kind.

We walked out in the backyard where my mother and sister waited. I remember the light was such that they looked almost as if they were floating there. We all climbed into my father's Chevy already cramped and crowded with a lamp my mother cherished, and her few plants, and some dishes we never used. My father said something small like "OK then, let's go," and that was it.

He started the car. I turned around as we pulled away. I wondered how, after we had moved so suddenly, anyone would ever find us again.

I hadn't been many places, so after driving a while I didn't recognize the streets anymore, or the buildings. I searched the faces we passed for someone familiar but it seemed that the farther we drove away from 30th Street, the less attached we were to the world, the less known somehow.

No one spoke on the drive across town. My father tuned the radio to a ball game. He said the name Garcia more than once under his breath, with some kind of satisfaction.

After what seemed like a slow drowsy dream that you can't quite shake off, he wheeled the Chevy finally into a side-yard parking lot where a two-story, four-family red-shingled apartment building loomed up. On one side of the apartment was the vacant lot that would become my forest, my wheat to harvest and my narrow passages; on the other side was St. Peter's Catholic Church. Dust was thick when he pulled the car into the yard. Already the grass was worn down to thin dirt. Beyond the side yard and the apartment building was a crumbling car barn where garbage was heaped and a junk car waited on blocks. I can still smell the garbage in the summer air, still hear the trains uncoupling in the rail yard nearby.

After a few minutes I walked out on a landing that led to the steep set of stairs we'd just climbed to get to our second-floor apartment. The summer light cut through the downstairs door and filled the stairwell. It was all newly painted in a deep shiny brown that was common in those days, especially in the kind of places where we lived.

Looking down the stairs I suddenly realized where we were, where I was: at the top of the landing I'd fallen from three years earlier. I shivered there for a second and clenched my fists and held my elbows tight against my sides as if to keep myself from falling again. I could feel myself leaning towards the edge of things.

I barely remembered the fall, but I remembered hanging on as I fell, and what had happened to my fingers and then the wild run in my father's arms to the doctor who had pulled the splinters out without anesthesia.

How could this be, I thought? Why were we back here? Why had we left 3oth Street to come again to this place of my falling?

I ran inside to find my father. He was standing in the newly painted kitchen showing something to my mother. He smiled when he turned to see me standing there with what must have been a look of stunned amazement on my face.

"You remember now, don't you?" he said. "You remember that we used to live here when you were a baby."

"Why are we moving back here now?" I asked. "Why did we have to leave Thirtieth Street and come back here?"

"I'm sorry I didn't tell you," he said. "But I knew you wouldn't like the idea and I wanted you to see how they'd fixed it up; don't you see how it's better now? They've fixed it up and painted it and rebuilt those stairs you fell down. I know you remember that."

I turned to look at my mother. I wanted to know more, or to know more deeply why this was happening, but she wasn't saying anything.

"You're so dumb," my sister said as she came into the kitchen. "Don't you know we don't have any money now, that Dad can't work now because they had to close his work down?"

I looked back at my father. He was smiling slightly and sweetly at me and he moved towards me. He picked me up and held me high above him as he had when I was a small boy.

"It's OK," he said. He turned to my sister and said that it wasn't true that we had no money, and that he'd be back at work as soon as they straightened out some things at the mill. He said he knew the man who owned this place, that it had been fixed up but was still a good and cheap rent.

"There's a lot of kids around here too," he said. "You'll like it, you'll see," and he put me back down.

I wanted to believe every word he said, so I stood there for a moment and played the words back through my brain.

My mother and father had already turned away and were putting our things into cupboards and closets and my sister was singing in another room, spinning her doll around in circles like a dance.

I walked out onto that landing again. I looked down those stairs but I was not afraid. I ran down the stairs and then back up again. I let my hand slide down the shiny brown banister. I ran up again trying to take two steps at a time. The stairs said nothing. They were only stairs and I was only a boy and things, I thought, would be all right.

23

I stepped out of my father's car onto the side yard driveway of the red apartment building that would be my home, and smelled the garbage and heard the trains uncouple, and I was released from one life and woke into a life I still don't fully remember entering. I was released too from a pressure that had made it hard for me to breathe sometimes; it had felt as if a snake was wrapped around me, like legs wrapped around me, squeezing my body until I thought I would cry out, or die.

One minute I was standing on the dusty side yard driveway looking up at the once-rotten second-story porch, my mother and my father and my sister near me, and the next minute I was alive in a way I had not yet imagined existed. I didn't know what to make of it then. Even now, I don't know what to make of it, except to say that there are portals, doors in the light that you may step through from one life to another.

The neighborhood around 17th Street all the way to Broadway on the east, and all the way to the lake on the north, was a haven for children those days. Thousands of us, the offspring of millworkers and assembly-line workers who'd fought a good war and come home to a country of promise and happy excess. Our parents were the children of immigrants, so they knew the value of place and they cherished it. We were the baby boomers, the milk of their good fortune, and we were all trapped inside a history that we didn't know existed but that spun us almost imperceptibly towards loss.

We were an army of children, roughly organized into divisions named for the compass points. You would say, for example, that you were from South Lorain, not just Lorain, or that you were from the East Side.

And these divisions too were divided, into the block or the street or the circle on which you lived. My boys and I were the 17th Street boys. These divisions were split into even smaller units that took the names of your adventures. We called ourselves the 17th Street Explorers; the Explorers for short.

I awoke in the company of the Explorers, amazed and happy I was among them, and before long I began to forget about 30th Street and the different lives we had had there. Although we had been suddenly wrenched out of one place and dropped down in another, that first 17th Street summer is among the happiest of my memories.

We arrived in the new neighborhood just as summer was taking shape, and blindly, as has almost always been my way, I stumbled into the current of things and found myself carried along. I know now that it was the first time I had been welcomed into a community, and the first time that others, other children and their parents, all of whom had been strangers to me, liked me and wanted me around simply for the little boy that I was.

As I drifted deeper into that life, into a way of being a self, a me, apart from my parents and family, I felt too that I was drifting further and further away from Sharon.

My parents still went out at night from time to time, but the people in the apartment building lived in what today we could call a communal way. That meant that no one locked their doors, that the four families borrowed and returned and borrowed again from one another—food and milk and tools and thread and clothes—and it meant that all of the adults took on an unspoken responsibility for all of the children. So when my parents went out, they would simply tell the man and woman who lived downstairs, some generous and comfortably sloppy West Virginians who parked their car on the lawn and cooked great generous noonday meals of pork and gravy and corn bread. My mother and father would ask them to keep an eye on us.

I think they almost always did, although my sister and I also came and went a lot more on our own. The neighborhood was safe for us in those days and within the boundaries we had come to learn from other children we could stay out later than we had in the past, and spend more time away from adults. So Sharon was never called again. I wondered for a long time if they somehow knew about us. More than once I tried to ask my mother, but whenever I'd bring up Sharon's name, my mother would change the subject or act as though she hadn't heard what I said.

"We don't need her anymore," she'd say. "You can stay here by yourself. Betty can keep an eye on you."

When I accepted that Sharon was gone, I felt an enormous relief. But soon after, I began to miss her in ways I couldn't even say then. At night I'd lie in my bed across the room from my sister (on 17th Street we had less room and shared a bedroom) and I'd let myself imagine that I was waiting for Sharon. Sometimes I could still feel my legs tighten the way they did when she sat on top of me during our wrestling and rocked herself fast and hard against me, breathing faster and faster, tossing back her head before she'd pull my pajamas open and lift her pleated skirt and pull her cotton panties off so she could rub herself against me.

"You can't tell no one," she'd say. "It's against the law."

I wondered even then what part of what we did was against the law, and I wondered what law it was we were breaking.

I could still feel that place I had always come to the threshold of but never crossed when she rubbed against me that way. I lay there needing her, although I couldn't say then that it was need, or want, or anything except a thing that called to me. And only when I'd see my mother and father get ready in their going-out clothes, and smell the TV dinners in the oven, did I feel that pull again, like a wire in my heart.

But the summer leaked out through the infinite blue of its sky, and the air got cool off the lake. We tried to make 17th Street our home again, and I let Sharon go. I believed I was safe in the world: that because this thing had happened to me, because I had done this thing and still went on living, I was removed from the world of hurt. I don't remember now why I believed I was protected in this way. I think I had it in my head that we each had only one large hurt to bear, and that if you could go on living after you got your particular hurt, there would be no more hurt like that again.

Part Four

Spike

24

In the early fall of that first year on 17th Street, my friend Walter from up the street got a nifty black dog. It was just a pup but it had a huge head and feet almost as big as mine. I liked the way the pup wrestled with us and bit our arms and hands with just enough force for us to feel the bite but not so much that it hurt, and that made me want a dog too.

My mother said we couldn't have a dog because the apartment was too small and on the second floor so the dog couldn't go outside. She said the dog would not be happy living here.

"But I'm happy here," I said. "Why couldn't a dog be happy?"

"It's too small," she said, "and besides, who'd take care of it?"

She said that when you had a dog, you had to feed it and walk it and give it water and take it to the doctor when it got sick.

I told her that I could do all of those things, that I was big now and could do things I couldn't do by myself before. I could tie my shoes by myself. I could fix my own breakfast when I got up and there was no one home, my mother and father working and my sister already out with her friends.

I thought about Sharon too, although I couldn't say the things I had learned there to help me convince my mother.

"Ask your father," she said when she got tired of listening to me beg.

So I shut up. I waited for him to come home. When he came home he took a bath first thing. The mill was a place of black dirt. I'd see him come in with a black fly-ash mask on his face, and even though he'd changed his clothes at work, I could still smell the slag all over him, and I would always know if it was the right time to ask him for something by the way he moved or by the presence of an occasional silence that I would come to fear. Sometimes when he came through the door in the kitchen where my mother was fixing supper, he had this way of grabbing her around the waist and half-lifting, half-spinning her around the small kitchen.

Afterwards he would walk into the bathroom and turn on the water in the tub. He would come out while the tub filled and take a bottle of beer from the refrigerator and sit at the small table and say, "What's up Bub" to me.

When he was like this I knew I could ask him what I wanted without fear, and even if his answer was no, he'd find a kind way to say it; he'd find a way to give me something else and not make it seem less than it was or less than the thing I'd wanted and I would soon forget about the thing I had really wanted and laugh along with him.

My father laughed when I told him I wanted a dog.

"Just another mouth to feed," he said. "Who the hell's gonna take care of a damn dog anyway?"

"I'll take care of him," I said, and my father laughed again and said he'd think about it and my mother said something under her breath from the stove, and my father got up to check his bath, the long-neck bottle of beer dangling from his hand.

25

When my father brought Spike home in a box, I was sitting near the coal stove with my sister. We came together there with our different lives, and sat near the stove to keep warm. He put the box down on the kitchen table. I saw it move and shake.

I want to say that my sister cried, that she ran behind our mother at the sink and pulled at her skirts, but it was me who cried when the box moved. I cried because even then I had seen the veil lifted a time or two. Even then I knew to fear things that moved inside of boxes your father brought home from the mill.

Spike was my dog when I was five. A ratty rattailed terrier with bent ears and a crazy dog grin. Some old man couldn't handle him anymore, so he gave him to my father. We had a small apartment then next to St. Peter's church with its outdoor rock altar and its blue bottomed holy pond, a grim four-family building where you had to share the bathroom with the drunk who sometimes would piss on the radiator in winter, a smell you could not wash away. When the old drunk would piss there in his drunkenness, my mother would wake to scrub it with a rough brush and lye soap. Even in winter she would open the window to let out the smell of human acids.

Three rooms and a bathroom you shared with strangers. Not a bad life, though I have always known a longing there, an emptiness I dwelled in even then.

When Spike hit the light of our kitchen where the coal stove sang and the family came together, it was as if a whirlwind had been released, a water spout or perhaps a small tornado. He spun his small tight muscle of a body all through the three rooms with such speed he was a blur. He ran so fast he seemed at times to run up the very walls, and he flew through the rooms so wildly that his running made them bigger, made us pause in our lives that had been headed somewhere else that night, somewhere not as bright or easy. We had already seen an empty table in that house, already we had felt the cold through cracks in the wall, but Spike somehow raised us above that grim life, above the mill noise and the slag dust. He caused us to look away from the sorrow and from the not having.

For a long time that night we could only stare, amazed. I had never seen a dog behave this way before. Nor had my father, who twice almost rose, I think to knock him down. Twice he almost rose. But after supper, after the mill noise lowered like a voice is quieted in the evening, Spike began to slow down, and as if to calm himself, he came to each of us and put his head in our hands, and like that he was inside of us.

Spike was my dog, but this is not the boy-and-dog story we're wont to tell. Not the noble dog who's taken from the boy in the city by evil men and delivered to hard labor in the cold. Not the dog who saves the boy from the fire, or from the well, or from the wild animal, or from the abandoned cave, or from the escaped con. Not that boy, and not that dog.

In the bedroom I shared with my sister, one window faced the street. Light from the church streaked in too. Two small beds only inches apart. A small dresser. Some shelves. One small light on a table between us. One small box for some toys. Autumn dusk, some yellow slag air on the rise. I'm busy at the toy box with a broken thing I'm trying to fix, sitting down facing the door, when dust suddenly shimmers in the light through the window, suddenly fills the light, and I see Spike between me and the door in a knot of shadows becoming something else. He begins to quiver and to jerk his head. He takes a wide stance and struts in the twelve-by-six-foot space between me and the door.

(I went back there once and troubled the poor people of those rooms to let me in. I stood in that room and felt it get smaller and smaller. They watched me shyly from the doorway. On the wall of the room where Spike had entered that other realm, they had a picture of Jesus Christ, glossy blood on his feet and hands; blood dripped from the crown of thorns, but no spirit of Spike, no boy, no residue of terror.)

Spike struts that wide stance and growls in a way I'd never heard him growl before, almost a human word comes out, almost a begging for release, and he whines high and painfully, and he makes a strange yelp too from time to time, and he jumps with all four feet in the air. But I am not afraid. Spike has never hurt me. He would never bite or scratch or snap at me. Not his boy, not even when I'd smacked him. Not even when I'd bitten him and shook his neck in my own mouth. I am not afraid. I only wonder why he moves in this strange way, and why that movement freezes me in place, my brain shutting things down on its own. Only when I see my father's face at the door, looking down at Spike, and then at me, do I know to be afraid.

"Don't move," he shouts, and Spike yelps like a spirit and jumps with all four feet so he makes me laugh. "Don't move and don't say nothing," my father shouts, and he shakes his fist at me, or at Spike.

I can't tell if he's mad at me in my dumb fear, unmoving, or at the dog, whose body is shaking and twitchy and making ugly yelps that must be wrong and bad. I can't tell until I see my father move towards me through the threshold with a grace I didn't know he possessed. He wants to lift me away, he says with his eyes, but Spike is at him like the spinning wild dog he had been the night my father brought him home, with that wild uncontrollable need.

My father jerks back when Spike does this, which makes me know a different terror: the one where the father is mortal. The one where the floodgates open to the world's bright debris. My father can only stand back in the hall, Spike stopped in the doorway, almost stilled in a slow rocking into himself, making quiet, low whines I think sound a lot like crying; they sound a lot like crying to me.

I entered another world then. A world of two small and terrible continents. Two small islands. On one I float in strange light with Spike. Distempered. Rabid, they said in those days. 1953, where Spike will not come towards me when I call him in all the voices that would usually make him come to me or hop and dance, or whine in song for scraps. He only wags his tail a bit when he hears his name, an act that must take unfathomable dog courage to call up from the spinning tunnel of his sickness.

On the other island is my father, and the whole rest of the world as I know it and care for it and want so badly to be among again. But Spike will not have it. I am his, and whenever my father tries to move towards me, Spike leaps, spit and snarl and yelp, from all fours like a toy dog, or like a dog in a cartoon, at my father's throat and drives him back into the hall. A ferocity like beauty.

"Don't move," my father says, and goes away.

26

Sometimes I feel free and light and brave as that boy I was by my toy box on that island of my sweet life, kept and claimed by the rabid dog who would not let anyone near, who even in his frenzy thought to keep them all away from me, his brain gone wrong except for that. Sometimes I want only to lie down and let it all go.

The time it took for my father to leave and return with a policeman close behind, I can measure only with the weight of need. Mine to simply sit there in my dullness and be the boy I was. Spike's to guard me hard and to the end.

The policeman has a steel bar. I think he'll hit the dog and make him stop, but instead he jabs the bar from the doorway at Spike's head as if to tease. In the policeman's eyes I see his fearful wonder, like in my father's eyes, and this makes me choke and gag. The policeman jabs the bar again until Spike snaps and the policeman pulls the bar away, dragging Spike by his clamped jaw.

I don't remember making words come. I don't remember caring for words, but I remember screaming *Stop* until Spike wags his tail again and almost turns around as if to drag up one more speck of memoried light, before he clenches down hard one last time on the bar and holds it in his rat dog's jaw.

Things move quickly now. I don't search for resolution anymore. What's done is done. I don't know why we long so for the dead who can do us no good.

The policeman drags Spike down the flight of dark stairs. My father follows. I'm left in the room, alone. I can't seem to stand or move until I hear a ruckus on the stairs. Even now, even to-night, with snow like a blanket over the broken day lilies, all of these lives and lives later, even now, I hear that snarling, snapping spit of a dog fighting for his life, and I hear the voices of the men too high in their panic. I run from the room towards the stairs and find my father behind the policeman who has Spike in a noose at the end of a long pole. He pushes Spike down. I grab my father's startled arm and hang on tight. He doesn't even hold me.

"Stay back," is all he says, and he pushes me away.

Outside the policeman holds Spike at bay at the end of the long pole. *That's what kind of trouble you can get into,* I think. He drags Spike towards the back where the garbage is heaped and the bro-ken cars commune. My father stands beside him when he takes his pistol out. No one looks to me on the porch. I watch the po-liceman take his pistol out, that lovely practiced move. No one looks to me on the porch. I am five years old, and I know enough. My father half turns his head away when the policeman draws the hammer back and squeezes off a round into the rat dog's brain.

This is the end of things, I think. Nothing can go on from this. No light would ever find us again. No peace could fill our hearts. No laughter near the coal stove with the wild dog who danced on his hind legs and turned a dancer's turn and fell and flew around the rooms for us. The end near the garbage heap. My ears ring-ing, I stand on the porch and let wash over me all the grief and fear and love that keeps blossoming, even now, inside me. World of hurt. Deepest, what remains.

Part Five

Sharon's October

27

I mourned that Spike dog for as long as I could. I tried to hold on to the body of him in my mind but he faded and I was left with the story of him instead, punctuated by that sharp report from the policeman's pistol when he fired the round into Spike's brain.

By early October, I had already moved on in my life, but I did not leave Spike behind, the way I had not left Sharon behind. I felt sometimes as if they were both strapped onto me and that I would have to carry them through my days. The only way I could be free of them was to bring them with me where they would be mostly silent and not worrisome. I would bring them out only at night, alone in my bed. Sometimes it felt as if they came out of my body and danced there before me in the dark. I know now that it was the story coming out of me; it was the story trying to tell me how to give it a life.

I was also happily distracted and excited about Halloween, and for weeks I had looked through Woolworth's and Kresges and Rexall with my mother, searching for a Lone Ranger costume.

The Ranger must have been out of favor, because the closest we came was a red-and-white cowboy suit with chaps and a plastic holster that made me look like a sissy when I tried it on over my street clothes in the drugstore bathroom.

There was the Zorro costume my mother argued for, which had a plastic sword with an open end fitted for a piece of chalk so you could mark those *Z*'s all over everything, and a cool, round black hat, and a cape.

Slashing that sword down the aisle and feeling the rayon cape sweep behind me, I wavered for a moment, but in the end I held out for the Ranger.

I had in my mind the first episode. I had in my mind the image of him lying almost dead in the grass, full of bullet holes from the men who'd ridden away quickly after the ambush. He was bleeding all over his body and not moving.

I had in my mind how his face looked when Tonto found him there by the river that he'd crawled to but couldn't quite reach. I wanted my face to look like that.

I had in mind the mask he made for himself, after Tonto nursed him back to health, so he could find his vengeance with the silver bullets and the white horse who rose up on his hind legs. He wanted to make things right in town again.

I don't know for sure if I had in mind Sharon too, her legs wrapped around me like the Ranger's around his white horse.

Wear the Lone Ranger pajamas, she'd say; *those are best for wrestling.*

It was my mother's idea to buy a black mask like his, and a white cowboy hat, and she even let herself spend money on a double-holster set: tin silver-studded black fake leather and white-handled silver six-guns with hammers that cocked, and a cylinder that turned a roll of caps that fired loudly and smoked.

I could hardly believe my luck. Until she paid with bills from the wallet she had deep in her purse and we turned away from the register to leave, I was afraid it was all too good; I was afraid that something would happen, that we'd get to the register and after the woman rang the numbers up, my mother would come to her senses and we'd have to give it all back.

But she paid, and I took the boxes and held them against my body and almost swooned with the thought of who I could be in that mask and white hat, wearing that double-holster set.

As we stood on the corner, waiting for our bus, my mother suddenly turned to me and said from out of nowhere, "And you can wear the Lone Ranger pajamas too, with your white pants over the bottoms, and I'll let you use my black gloves that Grandma bought for going out."

I closed my eyes and saw myself with all that gear. I knew I'd be quick on the draw. I knew that no one would ever ambush me again. I put my face against my mother's hip and held my boxes tight. The world was all before me.

28

My sister dressed as a cat in a costume that my mother had made from some kind of shiny black foundation garment. Out of cardboard painted black and fixed with a wire coat hanger, my father made the ears. He pulled six straws from the broom and painted them black too, to make the whiskers that he taped to my sister's face in a way that allowed them to move like a real cat's when she twitched her nose.

I was the Ranger through and through. I had put my gear on as soon as my mother and I got home the day before, and for a full evening and part of the next morning, I took my time and care to set it all right. I posed before the kitchen mirror until I found the perfect tilt of the hat, and the right place on my hips where the pistols should hang. With that mask on, in my Ranger pajama top and my white Ranger hat, twirling two silver pistols in my black gloved fingers, I was a thing to behold.

My mother gave us each a brown paper shopping bag with twine handles for our candy, and my father taught us a rhyme to say when the man or woman came to the door with a bowl of candy.

We are beggars from the street.
Shall we starve or shall we eat?

Walking down 17th Street towards Broadway and the neighborhood grown up around a large Catholic church, where we'd been told the rich people lived, my sister and I practiced the rhyme until we could do it in perfect unison.

We are beggars from the street.
Shall we starve or shall we eat?

I didn't know what it meant, really, although my sister tried to tell me. I remember only spots of time from that night, and although they are few, they are also hauntingly vivid and palpable. My sister tried to tell me what the rhyme meant but when I couldn't understand by the time we'd reached the first house, she gave up and said, "Just say the rhyme when they open the door. You don't have to know what it means."

As we walked up the long driveway of the first rich person's house, I said the rhyme a few more times to myself. I wanted to get the words right, even if I didn't know what they meant.

Sharon's October

We rang the bell and the door opened just a crack. An old woman stuck her head through the small opening as if to make sure we were trick-or-treaters and not someone after her money. When she saw that we were only kids, she opened the door. After we said our rhyme, she laughed out loud and very hard so that the loose skin under her chin shook, and she told us to come in.

I was afraid of her. She was dressed like a witch, in a tall pointed witch's hat and a strange, flowing, silky black dress. Although she didn't wear a mask, her face was thick with makeup of the kind that clowns use. She'd painted on a huge red downturned smile. Around her eyes she'd drawn a thick black line with fake eyebrows and fake eyelashes. At the end of her shockingly long, pointed and very real nose was a very real dark-colored wart. Just like a real witch, I remember thinking, and I looked at my sister to see if she was as worried as I was. I wondered if the woman was a real witch and, if she was, what she would do to us. Already, because of what had happened to me on 30th Street, I trusted no one.

The three of us stood in a long, dark hallway lit only by a candle inside an enormous and frightening jack-o'-lantern she had set on the floor. On a table in the hall behind the witch I saw a bowl of candy. The witch laughed again when she saw me eyeing the candy and said, "You can have all you want, but first you have to tell me who you are."

"I'm a cat," my sister said, as if that were not apparent.

The witch laughed again and said, "I know you're a cat, but what cat are you? What's your name? Who do you belong to?"

My sister looked at me as if I could answer for her, or as if to say *Let's get out of here.* Questions weren't supposed to be part of the bargain. My father and mother had spent hours putting our costumes together, they'd taught us the rhyme to say, but they hadn't said anything about questions.

"I'm just a cat," my sister said. "I don't have a name. I belong to my mother and father."

The witch told her that all cats had names and asked my sister what her name was.

"Cheryl Weigl," she said. "I live in Lorain."

"OK then," the witch said, "your cat name is Cheryl Weigl from Lorain, and what a great cat name it is!"

I was ready when she turned to me. "I'm the Lone Ranger," I told her before she could ask. "I've got two silver six-guns and my horse Silver is waiting outside. Tonto saved me after I got shot."

As the witch laughed out loud again, I thought it sounded like Sharon's strange laugh and I could not help but think about Sharon.

Wear the Lone Ranger pajamas, she would say. Still I wore them.

The witch finally led us to the bowl of candy and after we'd each taken a few pieces she said, "No, take more. Take as much as you want."

Again we were presented with a problem that our mother and father had not prepared us for. I looked up at the witch. Her wart seemed to have gotten bigger, and in the candlelight flickering off the white walls of the hallway, she looked more and more like a real witch. I reached into the bowl with both hands and grabbed as much candy as I could hold. I dropped the candy into my bag and before my sister could take more for herself, I did the same again and looked up at the witch.

"That's right, Lone Ranger," she said, "take as much as you want. You'll need all of your strength."

I didn't know what she meant but I didn't like the sound of it. I'd come to mistrust adults who talked in circles, who said things in a way that made them sound as if they were thinking something else. I told her I had enough candy and told my sister to take some more so we could leave.

After my sister took a single handful and dropped it into her bag, we both turned to walk back out of the door.

"Good-bye, Cheryl Weigl Cat from Lorain," the witch said. "Good-bye, Lone Ranger. Don't forget to tell Tonto and Silver I said hello."

Down the street under a streetlight we opened our bags and dug into the candy in spite of our father's warning not to eat anything until we'd gotten home. We ate a few candy bars that we knew would be safe because they were still in their wrappers, and we made our way up the long block of big houses, crossing the street now and then to knock on the door of a house that looked particularly promising.

After only an hour or so our bags were more than half full and we knew we had found the mother lode. Our old neighborhood had been nothing like this. You'd get an apple back there, or some homemade caramel corn, or maybe a penny candy. But here, among the people who owned the stores and worked in the banks, every house was a different indulgence. One man, who came to the door dressed in a gorilla suit, even gave away shiny new dimes hidden inside small bags of candy he'd wrapped in silver paper.

29

We ate well along the way. Our bags were filled and our pockets stuffed with candy so we decided to head for home. We had walked quite a distance but I knew the way. I told my sister that I knew a shortcut and led her along the railroad tracks, past a row of warehouses and out into an open field that bordered the opposite side of our street.

The sky was rent with stars. You could see the small beams of flashlights from other children out trick-or-treating, darting here and there through the dark neighborhood trees. A siren whirled towards some trouble. I tried to pick out the lights of our apartment across the field when I noticed something else, something to my left.

Just beyond the edge of the trees that bordered the field behind us and to our left I saw a huge house lit up like downtown. In every window was a small plastic jack-o'-lantern with a light inside. I stared at the house because it seemed to call to me. I told my sister that we should make one more stop. I pointed across the field to the house, all lit up, and told her that it looked like they probably gave good candy there.

"We've got enough already," she said, "and it's late. We'd better get home."

"It's so close," I said. "Let's just go to that house and then we can go home."

She relented and we walked through the field towards the house. The closer we got, the more. I felt as if I'd been there before, or that I knew someone there, although surely I had never been there and didn't know anyone who lived in such a big house. My sister was wary of the time so we hurried.

"You knock," she said, "and you sing the rhyme; I'm too tired."

I rang the bell hard a few times and stepped back to get ready to sing our beggar's song.

When the door opened and I looked up at the face of the woman who'd come to give us candy, it was as if someone had punched me in the stomach. I was almost knocked backwards off the porch.

I know that I did stumble, because I remember my sister laughing as I tried to gain my balance. I remember my sister grabbing my arm.

"Sing the song," she said under her breath.

But I could only stare up at the woman's face. First I was filled with unimaginable terror and shame. I wondered what Sharon would say or do when she recognized me.

Then, almost immediately, an odd, warm calm came over me when I remembered I had a mask on. Instantly the terror returned when I remembered that although I was in a costume, my eyes covered by the black mask, it was the Ranger's costume, and the Ranger's mask, and what showed most clearly was the top of my old Ranger pajamas that Sharon had liked me to wear.

When it became clear to my sister that I couldn't or that I wouldn't sing the song, she sang it for us.

We are beggars from the street.
Shall we starve or shall we eat?

I heard the song as if through a long tunnel, far away from the sound of my sister's voice. When I tried to concentrate on Sharon and on my sister, retrieving the candy Sharon handed through the door, my eyes blurred and I couldn't focus; instead of seeing what I knew was before me—a woman, standing in her open doorway, passing candy out to me and my sister—I saw scenes from that other time, that time with Sharon in the living room on 30th Street, and I could feel myself being rocked as I lay on top of her, the motion of our rocking causing my head to spin, making me sick to my stomach.

My ears rang too so I couldn't hear anything clearly. The world seemed to be rushing past me at blinding speed and it was all I could do to hang on.

Just at the moment I thought I would be sucked away into a swirling black tunnel, I felt my sister's hand on my arm, pulling me off the porch and down the porch steps.

"Let's go," she said. "What's wrong with you?"

Not until we were back in the empty field and well away from Sharon's house did I begin to feel safe. My sister was still tugging at my arm.

"What happened to you back there? Why were you acting that way?"

I looked closely at her face to see if I might find at least a hint of the terror I felt, but she only looked puzzled.

"Do you know who that was?" I said.

"It was Sharon," she said, "our old baby-sitter. That's what we were talking about on the porch when you were acting so stupid. She kept asking me what was wrong with you, why you wouldn't say anything. She said she liked your costume. What *is* wrong with you?"

"Did she say anything else?" I asked.

"What do you mean? She just asked why we were trick-or-treating so far from 30th Street, so I told her that we moved."

"Did you tell her where we lived now?"

"Yeah, I told her we lived on 17th Street, just on the other side of the field, but she already knew. Why? What's wrong? Why are you acting so weird?"

I couldn't explain. She knew nothing, or at least remembered nothing, about my nights of Sharon. It was too late to try to tell her all of it now. I felt a kind of grief because I thought if I did try to tell her, she'd never believe me, and that made me wonder if anyone would ever believe me.

"I'm OK," I said. "I just ate too much candy. Let's go home now."

30

When we came in, my father had the small coal stove blazing in what we called our big room because it was the living room and kitchen together. I felt the heat wash over me when I walked through the door.

"How'd ya do?" he asked. "Did you say your rhyme?"

We held up our bags and he applauded. My mother said she couldn't imagine what we would do with all of that candy.

"We'll eat it," my father said, and then he laughed.

I begged off going through the ritual of checking the candy with my father and sister. I risked getting smacked for disobeying when I told him that I had a stomach ache from eating too much already.

"That's what you get for not listening," he said, "now go to bed."

Once under my covers I could hardly contain myself. I squinted my eyes shut hard to try to find Sharon's face and keep it there. I think I must have swooned. I was flushed and filled with nervous twitching. I could hear the voices of my people in the big room as they sorted through the candy. I could hear them when they laughed. I tried to listen for my sister mention Sharon, but she didn't.

For a while I thought to myself that I would try to put it all together in my head and figure out if Sharon's being here, so close to us, meant anything, but I couldn't concentrate. My mind kept flying back to the living-room floor on 30th Street where we had done our wrestling, and then to the porch of Sharon's house where my sister and I had waited tonight with our bags of candy, and then back to 30th Street again, great sweeping flights that made my stomach churn. After a while I saw the apartment's lights go out through the crack under my door and I heard the going-to-bed sounds of my mother and father. I wanted sleep to be a thing that would come and take me into its arms. I took my six-guns off but wore the rest of my costume. I curled up into myself, full of remembering.

31

After supper the next day I stood up and told my mother and father that I was going outside to play.

I hung around the yard for a few minutes, then walked towards St. Peter's. I threw some stones in the holy pond and looked back at the apartment to see if anyone else had come outside or was looking out of the window.

Trying to look like I was only a wandering boy, I walked through the field towards a tree line behind Sharon's house. I think I needed to account for the longing that had grown inside me since I had last been with her. Maybe there was something I could see over there at her house, something that would help me understand. Or maybe I didn't know why I was there, or what I was doing. I don't know now, either.

I crouched behind some bushes thirty yards from Sharon's back door. Cold air off the lake made me shiver. I tried to make myself more comfortable by sitting down and pulling my knees up to my chest. Without thinking about it, I resolved to wait there until I saw her.

Just as the gas streetlights began to flicker on, I saw a car pull up in Sharon's driveway. I leaned in the direction of her house and squinted to focus on the people getting out.

I saw her then, and again felt that stinging in my legs. After Sharon and the others had gone inside I stood up to go home. I looked back once more at her house, all lit up like it had been the night before, the jack-o'-lanterns still in the windows. It was almost dark, and I knew I had to get home, but I could not keep myself from walking towards her house, although I didn't know what I would do there.

I don't know why I wasn't afraid. I stood straight up and walked to a place behind a small shed off the end of the driveway. I could see people now, moving around behind the lit-up windows. I put my mouth against the rough wood of the shed wall and felt that swooning again. I scanned the place and saw a knot of shadows to one side of the house under what looked like the kitchen window. I made my way there and stood for a few minutes, trying to figure out where Sharon's room might be. Lights came on and then were turned out. It was so quiet that I could suddenly hear my father's voice from the other side of the field, calling my name. I walked around the house, carefully looking up into each dark window. On the side opposite the field, I came to an open window from which music leaked. I got as close to the window as I could. The room was as dark as the others except for a small light that someone crossed back and forth before, making nervous shadows on the wall. I concentrated on the music. I was close enough to hear the words. It was a song about a lion sleeping in the jungle, and someone telling a baby not to cry.

32

All through that fall and most of the winter I took my good time in the shadows of Sharon's house. I went there so often and so deviously that I learned the best times and the best places to hide where I would see the most.

Crouching there under the windows after dark those evenings, I felt naked, but it was a nakedness I came to long for; it was the nakedness I had felt those nights in my bed, waiting for Sharon to come and bring me into the television's blue light.

I don't remember now how many times I went there, but I went enough to have seen Sharon's body more than once through the bathroom window when she climbed out of the tub; I went enough times to see her dance in the backyard when she came out so suddenly she almost scared me into screaming. I managed to hide behind the shed. She stood to one side of the house and looked back at the door a few times before lighting a cigarette. She had a small transistor radio that she held up to her ear with one hand; in the other she held a cigarette, whose red tip traced lines in the dark as she danced. She moved those hips that I had known in a loathsome way that I imagined for a moment was for me.

I went there at least those many times. It must have been enough because the wheel of the world began to turn again, and I eventually stopped going there altogether.

I knew that I could not forget her, but I had lost my longing for her. Something inside me had grown a little harder since those days on 30th Street. Somehow the powerful need and shame I had felt for Sharon became a more simple pleasure in my mind. I could call on it at any time and conjure the image of her sitting on top of me, her pleated skirt pulled up, her underpants pulled down around her ankles.

Depending on how long I wanted to let it go, I could make her start to rock, there in my head, and once I got that good at remembering, she was mine. I could hold her as long as I wanted to inside the story of my life.

Part Six
The Borderline

33

For more years than I can recall, the seasons after that autumn seemed to collapse into one long stretch of days that I felt more and more removed from. I don't know if I always felt this distance from the world, or if it started after Sharon, but I know that it's been with me for a long time; although there's a part of me that hates it, I would smash anything that tried to say it could be otherwise.

This detachment eventually distanced me from my family. I became a fiercely independent boy, holding down jobs around the neighborhood even before I'd stopped wetting the bed, cutting grass in the summer and shoveling snow in the winter for a list of regular customers. I had my own cash in my pocket and I pretty much came and went as I pleased. I had friends too. We played baseball and football and simple-minded games of war. We hung out by the river or crawled under the fence of the steel mill to climb the slag heaps where we'd smoke and sometimes touch ourselves.

Mostly, though, I tried to be by myself, and to play the silent games I had invented that always starred me as the hero, saving someone from some kind of trouble to be loved by the many. I would make a kind of crowd-cheering noise into my cupped hands as they presented me with my medal. It went on and on this way until it became my life. I wanted someone to save me from it, but I did not know how to ask.

What finally did save me was the time I spent with my maternal grandparents, which had started when I was nine or ten regular sleepovers once or twice a month. After a while I started staying over on the weekends sometimes, but never with my sister. I loved Anna and Ivan Grassa like I loved my own mother and father, and I have come to see how much they meant to me only as the years after their deaths have piled up and the stories they gave me have begun to take the place of those lives that have passed.

I don't think they knew they were giving me the gift of the story powerfully enough to change my life, but I believe they knew it was a way to stay with me long after they'd gone.

My earliest stays there would be short, so I knew I'd eventually go home, but long enough so I knew there was more going on than my parents' weekend trips.

Years after the longer sleepover visits had stopped, I would ask my mother and my father why I had stayed there, but always I got the runaround. It seemed that the further we got away from those visits, which must have stopped when I was in my early teens, the less real they became to the rest of my family, until one day the long visits stopped existing for everyone except me, as if I had made them up.

After that point, being in the presence of such staunch, unwavering denial of the times that I remembered so clearly would cause me to feel like I might lose my mind, or even sometimes like I was the target of a conspiracy contrived by my mother and father to protect me from something they felt I couldn't bear.

By my late teens I stopped asking about those times I had spent with my grandparents, but I have never forgotten them. I told those stories to myself over and over, the way my family told their stories to one another, so I would remember them. I knew they were real, and telling them that way, even to myself, because there was no one else to listen, made them more real. The stories enabled me to live beside my grandparents inside the memory of a long chain of summer evenings stretched out over three or four years.

Occasionally, sitting around with my family, I'd catch my mother and father unaware and I would start into one of the stories. I'd get some crucial detail wrong on purpose, and they'd correct me. My plan was to draw them into the telling somehow and thus expose the reality of my memories and their conspiracy to keep them from me.

My mother or father would always chime in with a more precise rendering of the story, telling me what I'd gotten wrong. I'd pause a long time then and look at them. I'd let their telling linger in the air as if to settle it into being. Then I'd say, "See, you do remember; that happened during one of those times I stayed with Grandma and Grandpa, one of those long visits in the summer when you and Cheryl would disappear and I'd be left with them."

Their quietude and drowsy countenance would suddenly be transformed into agitation. They would start sputtering answers that made no sense.

"You don't know what you're talking about," my father would say, then look at my mother.

"You just heard Grandpa tell that story at our house," my mother would add, "or you heard him tell it when we were all there. You know he loved to tell stories. I don't know why you imagine you stayed there. Why would we lie? Why would we say you hadn't stayed there if you had?"

I knew she didn't want me to answer, but I did anyway.

"That's the real question," I'd say. "I don't know why, but I know I stayed there. I have the stories to prove it. I saw things that you didn't see, and heard things from them that they never told to anyone but me. If you know those same things now, you heard them from me when I was a kid, so they have to be real."

"You're crazy," my father would say, and he'd laugh it off and the conspiracy would begin again, and then we'd drink a drink and I'd let it all go.

34

I have never let the stories go. I am blessed with the stories that the world gave me through my grandmother and grandfather.

The earliest story that I remember my grandfather telling me has to do with the birth of my mother. I was young enough to still be frightened by some of the details, and I would lie in bed beside my grandmother those nights, fearing the story. It was this story that, more than anything else, contributed to how I saw my grandfather Ivan from the time I was a child until this very night. It was a story that shaped him in my mind in a way that would never change, even after the many strokes that took him away from us, piece by piece.

My mother was the first of two daughters born to Ivan and Anna. My grandfather said they'd planned on having the baby in the hospital because that's where people had babies in America, but he got home late one night after working midshift—which ended at eleven—then stopping for a late beer at a bar on Broadway, to find my grandmother deep in labor. He didn't have a car and he didn't know anyone nearby who did. He called the doctor but the doctor's wife answered, saying her husband was out. My grandfather tried to explain the urgency, tried to say in his broken English that my grandmother needed the doctor *now*, that the baby was coming and he didn't have a car to take my grandmother to the hospital.

When he told this story, Ivan Grassa always shook his head when he came to this part, and he swore something in Serbo-Croatian that translates roughly as *May the devil take your skin.*

"This was my baby coming," he would say then, "and the goddamn son-of-a-bitch doctor's wife doesn't give a shit."

"'Kiss my ass,' I say to her; 'tell me where your goddamn doctor husband is or my baby will die and my wife with it.'"

He finally scared her into telling him that her husband was at the Slovak Club, playing cards as he did every Wednesday night. Ivan Grassa hung up the phone with another curse. The Slovak Club was right around the corner so instead of calling and having to go through the same thing with the doctor, Ivan ran out the door to bring the doctor back.

My grandmother would stop smiling now in the story. She'd make a hissing sound and shake her head. "It was late, and raining, and he went out without a coat. He left me by myself," my grandmother would say. "This was my first baby. I didn't know what to do with the hurt. It felt like the baby wanted to come but was stuck."

Ivan ran the two blocks to the Slovak Club and pounded on the door for a long time because you had to have a member's key to get in. Finally someone came out and asked Ivan what he wanted.

"I need the goddamn doctor," he said. "My baby is coming now and I need the doctor."

The man at the door tried to tell Ivan to wait, but he pushed past and barged into the private bar where five men were playing cards at one of the tables.

Again Anna would shake her head and make the hissing sound. "In the rain he went out, no coat, or hat, or anything," she recalled.

Ivan knew right away that the doctor was drunk or nearly drunk, that they'd been playing cards for hours by then and drinking all along.

"I didn't say nothing," he said. "I grabbed the son-of-a-bitch by the collar of his fancy jacket and pulled him up and dragged him to the door." One or two of the other men playing cards stood up as if to try to stop him but Ivan believed they must have seen the crazy thing in his eyes, and they sat back down.

"Where's your goddamn bag," Ivan asked as he dragged the doctor out. "In the car," the doctor said, so Ivan dragged him out in the rain where they fetched the bag.

The doctor wanted to drive but Ivan refused, saying, "Too much time to start the car, we can run." But the doctor was drunk and he stumbled at least twice and Ivan had to pick him up.

"I could smell the whiskey on him when he came through the door," Anna would remember. This was never her story, except for a word here and a word there, which Ivan paused to allow.

The doctor examined my grandmother and said the baby was coming but was turned the wrong way, that he had to take her to the hospital.

"But your grandmother is screaming now," Ivan would say to me. He told the doctor, *"No. No time. Do it now. Do it here."*

The doctor opened his bag. Ivan said the doctor's hands were shaking by then, that he was so drunk he could barely find what he needed.

"Now I'm afraid," Ivan would tell me. "What can I do? He's drunk and the baby is stuck and your grandmother is screaming." He left the doctor to go to the basement and get his gun, a pistol his brother had smuggled from Zagreb. He came back upstairs with the gun to find the doctor kneeling on the bed over Anna, his right hand deep inside of her.

"The son-of-a-bitch is drunk. I don't think he knows what he's doing. I don't know how to save my baby so I stood above them and held the pistol that Streetz brought from Zagreb to the doctor's head. I told him that if the baby died, or if your grandmother died, that he would die right there beside them."

Hearing this story as a boy, I knew no one had died, but I was still frightened when he told it that way. He held the pistol to the doctor's head the whole time. In his drunken fear the doctor cut my newborn mother badly, and twisted her leg so hard and awkwardly that he pulled it out of her hip socket. Today my mother still limps from this, her one hip canted at an odd angle as if she were walking on a slope.

"She was covered with blood from the son-of-a-bitch cutting her," Ivan would say, "but she was alive. We wrapped your mother in a blanket and I kicked the son-of-a-bitch back out into the rain. I kicked him in his ass to shame him. I should have shot the son-of-a-bitch right there, in the alley, but your mother and your grandmother were alive. I didn't know that he'd ruined her leg forever so I let him go.

"Son-of-a-bitch doctors," Ivan would say, then lie back in his chair and sigh a heavy sigh to let you know the story was over.

Since the first night I heard that story, I have always seen my grandfather that way: soaked from rain and sweat, his pistol held to the doctor's head while my grandmother screamed. I see him that way in my mind and I think that is what love means, Ivan's gun pointed at the doctor's head to save his wife and his baby.

35

After the many small and large strokes had torn him apart, piece by piece, I would go to his house to see him. Sometimes I helped my grandmother bathe him with soft rags or brought him his whiskey in the evening while she said her rosary before the crucifix and dried palm leaves on the wall. He couldn't stand by himself by then, or walk, or even lift his arms. He didn't know his children or grandchildren who came to his bed to hold his swollen hands and kiss his face. He slept in a daybed where my grandmother said the sun could find him, and the toilet wasn't far when she had to carry him there to piss because he could not hold it up himself. She would hold it for him as I imagined she had in love when they had tumbled together into the same bed. Those days I could not help but watch him linger in the consuming shock of his brain assaulting itself, as he called out from time to time in the language he had never abandoned to the old country dying out in his heart.

Sometimes I would watch Anna shave him. She stropped the razor, brushed up the lather and shaved him with such grace that he wouldn't bleed. She had started sleeping on the hard couch to be near him in the night. She kept a flashlight on the table beside her so she could shine the light under her blankets when he demanded to see that no other man was sleeping with her.

I spent long hours there during one of those times in my life when I had stepped through a portal and was struggling to get back into the world, but my grandfather did not know who I was.

The day I had left for the war almost a year earlier, I had driven through the snow to his house to say good-bye in my uniform. He was sick by then but still pretty sharp, and I could tell he was proud of me. We drank a shot together and I told him I had to leave. As I walked away after kissing him good-bye, he tripped me with his cane.

During my year in the war he had his worst stroke. After that, whenever he saw me, he'd ask, "Where is the soldier?"

"I'm the soldier, Grandpa," I'd say. "I used to be a soldier."

He'd look at me with such a lost look that I wanted to lie to him.

"No," he'd say, "where's the one who's the soldier?"

36

My grandfather was a Yugoslav in this century of blood and cruel armies. His name was Ivan Grassa from Zagreb, son of a farmer and a trader of horses who sent my grandfather away from war to America. The night before my grandfather said his long good-byes, his father had the butcher tattoo a watch on my grandfather's wrist with the time his steerage would unbind its lines and sail, not to a new world, just a different one. Three o'clock, the watch said.

"Three o'clock," Ivan Grassa would say when we asked for the time. And always he would look at the faded blue watch, and tap his fingers on the watch face.

My grandfather had told me the story of his departure from the time I was a boy, how he had left the house one dawn with his father and walked across the pasture to the railroad tracks and followed them to the station. He told me this first on his lap, on the screened porch with its cot where he napped in the afternoons. He told me different versions throughout my life. I thought the way the story changed from year to year, from telling to telling, was how stories were meant to be told. I thought, *Someday I'm supposed to do something with this.* And later, when I was old enough, we would drink together in the bars of sweet Lorain (how good

that was with my old Ivan Grassa) and he would tell me the different versions. Sometimes women were involved—trouble with a
girl's father—or sometimes trouble with the Army. We drank
shots and beers after hard work laying a new sidewalk in front of
his small house and he would tell me the story.

He had walked across the pasture, he said, with his silent father in the breaking dawn, to the station. The two rode, still not
speaking, in a crowded common car to the docks. He said his father turned away without waving. He said he spread his blanket
out on deck and hid his money in his crotch. I have seen him do
this. I have seen him through a fog or mist hide his wallet this way.

We had shoveled and sweat the whole morning and half the
afternoon, busting up old sidewalk and laying new. He stood over
me with his cane and pointed me through his way of doing the
work. We had built the forms with boards he'd rough-cut from a
fallen plum tree years before and then had stored in the dark, damp
inner sanctum of his pigeon coop. They were badly gnarled, but
he showed me how to soak them with water from the bucket and
bend them straight between stakes.

"You keep the things you have," he said. "You make the things
you have work."

I did what I was told in those days. I worked hard with my back
because work was in my soul. I was built for digging holes. After
the good work, after cold sausage on black bread and some cheese,
we went to drink together.

I don't think I was alive enough then. I know it's wrong to long
so for those who have gone, but if I could live more fully now, I'd
choose to stand in that light with him again. I'd linger on every
detail of the way he tried to show me.

Ivan Grassa owned a small plot of land and a shingled brown
house in America, where he dreamed his way as a boy with a watch

tattooed on his wrist and whiskey on his lips. His neighbor was Vlagio from Poland, who owned another small plot, bought, I think I can say, with the sweat of his brow. Over the borderline between their backyards, for forty years, they fought.

This is not a metaphor. They fought about who owned the land between their yards. They had it measured, and surveyed, and staked again and again as if the world could have somehow shifted and given the other some inch or two of advantage; as if it were possible to hold a piece of earth only inches wide. Like that the years went past.

And my grandmother, Anna from Jlubiana, who was closer to God than thou, planted lilies where Ivan had pointed with his cane, lilies that the other man dug up in the night, where he had waited like a thief. Anna planted lilies on the borderline and nearby, next to the alley; she planted a garden with leafy lettuce like huge green fans or flags unfurled, and garlic big as your fist, and a few red potatoes, and some peppers yellow-hot. She had come at sixteen to Ellis Island with her papers around her neck, and her crucifix, and her confirmation scapular. She told me this story the morning of my own confirmation, and she put a piece of rock candy in my mouth and held me when my candle snapped in the holy procession and I cried. She prayed at Mass with Father every morning in the St. Vitus Church she loved for its Virgin. She lit candles and kept vigil for the dead.

They had met in a boardinghouse in Lorain. Years later at Anna's wake in the basement of the funeral home, a woman told me this story of my people. She was the child of the people who had owned the boardinghouse back then. The Father sat across from us and ate, listening in silence, and sometimes nodded. He had married my mother and father. He had baptized me, first put the host to my lips, and delivered me to the fat bishop who I swear cut gas when I knelt to kiss his ring in confirmation.

The Father had also come to Ivan and Anna's house on Livingston Avenue to write the Latin blessings in chalk above the threshold, and he came once a month to cut Ivan's hair after Ivan's first stroke, and to hear his sins (there were none), and to give him the body and the blood of Christ though he surely knew what Ivan Grassa thought of Christ. My grandfather never went inside a church after his wedding and the christening of his daughters. He cursed the Pope and praised the Gypsies and swore with what he called his devil's tongue.

This woman who had known my grandparents was seventy now, the old world laid over her like a surplice, her eyes lovely when she remembered the girl my grandmother had been, coming to work for them in the boardinghouse, and my grandfather coming too, later, to take a room alone and to work the three shifts of the mill that sang the steel out nearby.

My grandmother mopped the halls and bathrooms, the woman said. She mopped the toilets and wrung out the mop full of piss over the banister in the back above the alley. The woman who was the child of the boardinghouse family told me this story in the basement of the funeral home at the wake of my grandmother so that I might see my grandmother as she was then.

She ate some of the sausage on her plate, slowly. She seemed to want me to be in a place where I could hear her most clearly. She said that she remembered one day when my grandmother walked from the toilet with a mop full of piss, and Ivan Grassa, who ran a crane in the mill and who lived in the house by himself and drank the evenings into nothing, jumped out from a hidden place and grabbed Anna's crotch. He had been watching her, the woman said. He had his eye on her. In Zagreb, this gesture was a sweet endearment back then, but my grandmother whirled and slapped the piss-heavy mop across Ivan Grassa's face until he let go of her.

The woman told the story while we ate the food of the wake prepared by the Slovenian women of the church who are old now too, daughters of immigrants, ghosts alive in their eyes.

This mop of piss across his face, his hand around her sex, I had heard my grandfather say more than once, was why he chose Anna for his wife.

I watched the Father eat and fall back into memory. I thought some force would hold us all together back then, the desperate lives we were, and tonight I am fearing or hating myself like I watched them hate each other, my grandfather and his good neighbor from Warsaw, who had his own immigrant's bundle like a hump on his back. They hated each other so long and so deeply their hate became a love for how they tended it with care and shaped it into a way of being they despised but could not let go.

I don't know if I can say this right. Always I am of two minds, but it feels as if they were acting out that need that sometimes takes us to hurt someone because we think it makes us better, although it's only ourselves we want to hurt. We want to hurt ourselves because no one loved us, or because no one loved us enough, or because no one loved us in the right way, or because someone killed the love somehow with a belt, or with a bottle, or with their sex. I can only say it one way. I have only words.

All of my growing up I heard these men fill the air with their curses and stand fast at the borderline no matter what, as if the small backyards were ancient countries. I stood under the plum tree watching and listening. Watching and listening, stuck from time to time in a dumb reverie, hearing my grandfather and his

Vlagio, whom he loved to hate and curse. I thought then that I would have them forever, but everything moves away, continuously, like the sky.

I call for the spirits to come down, those wings who long to beat inside a life. I'm calling their names. The night presses in at the door this very instant. The night with all its blackness presses in. I'm calling their names so they may return to claim the common ground, the blood spilled there, the sweat, the slit-throat chickens of the yard, the blue pigeons of our desire, the dandelions at the borderline under leaves in spring that Anna picked for her salad.

37

I passed into adolescence and a long time of no words. I passed into a silence that I struggled against, a silence that was so powerful I could sometimes not even say my own name to someone who asked it.

Now sometimes I am so full with words that they stream out of me like a language I never learned but can still speak in my dreams. Other times it's as if my tongue has been purged of the words, like the prophet's tongue, by the hot coal of godly chastisement. I have lived so long with words that they sometimes lose their meaning, a curse and a blessing.

Tonight, a waxing and hazed-over early autumn moon, ubiquitous as loss, called me finally back to words. I watched that moon come up on its track of stars and that moon sent me to this story because I could see the rivers there, cut into the rock like scars old as time.

A long time ago, I walked through one of those portals, one of those doors that have always seemed to lead me to understanding. I have difficulty remembering the order of things since that passage. Time got stupid to me. The borders between the before and the after became blurred or seemed to disappear so that I found myself caught in a swirling immediacy where everything seemed to happen at once.

Because sometimes I could not remember the sequence of my life and of the lives of those around me, I had to lie. I had to invent a way of seeing the world as I imagined others saw it so that I might live among them.

There was no longer a past for me, or a future. Sharon and Spike and my falling stairs all existed in the same precise moment that played over and over in my mind and that connected all moments with all other moments in a timelessness. I tried to find a way to understand my life. I had done so much traveling in the world of hurt that had been my life that the boundaries we need in order to be human had vanished. I had invented new boundaries. I invented the before and the after.

For a while the words would not let the story come. The words conspired against me so my fingers could not make the pencil move. I let the many small indignities and the many small betrayals fester too deeply inside me. For a while, I let the evil have its way with me. I found myself in a world that didn't know me. I was tongue-tied and stunned by the horror and by the beautiful dying until the story came again to save me.

Part Seven

Before and After

38

I want to tell you now about how hard it was to come home. I want to tell you about how lonely we were in our own country.

There was and there was not a before and an after.

I want to tell you about how our sisters stopped speaking to us, how our mothers and fathers were afraid because we slept in different rooms each night after we had come home, and because we would leap at a person's throat if a hand reached to touch us in our sleep.

I want to tell you how it feels to stroll in a common zone among the people of your life after war.

I want to tell you about the faith that it takes to come back and be among the sweetly uninitiated, and to live as if calm or sane.

Coming back to America, which I still loved in 1968, was like returning to a foreign land. During my year in the war I had changed in ways I was only beginning to understand, but I was not prepared for how my country had changed, for how my people had changed, a softness, which I don't even know if I had imagined, gone from their eyes.

I didn't know much in 1968; the war had burned a hole in my brain. Still, I could sense that something distant and terrifying had happened to us that would change us forever.

I would not have used the word consciousness then, but that's what I meant. I would have said that it was more a change in the way the world looked to us out of our windows, the horizon slightly tilted, things out of whack so that none of the old moral reference points could sustain us. We had seen and given and taken blood. You can't fix that with words.

One day I was squatting down in a bunker, stoned on Vietnamese dope so rich that it stained my fingers with its resin, waiting out a rocket attack, and two days later I was standing in the knickknacked living room of my parent's house, breathing the old air.

No one spit on me when I walked through the San Francisco Airport to book a flight to Cleveland, that day I tried to come home, although, like you, I have heard those stories. I don't know what I would have done; spit back, I suppose. I was jumpy. Standing in line before the ticket counter, I fell to the carpeted floor when some kid threw an empty soda can a few feet from where he sat into a metal trash can.

People looked me up and down until they must have made the connection. They must have watched their televisions during supper and seen at least a part of what had gone on in our Republic of Vietnam, an image or two of someone dying, or of someone who wanted to die; they must have seen part of what had gone completely out of control there. I picked myself up from the airport carpet unashamed, happy that the soda can's bang hadn't been small-arms fire, or mortar rounds that the VC walked in on us as we slept under guard of the trees.

I had landed a few hours earlier at Oakland on a civilian flight that had circled the airport for thirty minutes, waiting for the fog to clear. I could almost not bear those thirty minutes. From the moment we'd taken off from Tan Sa Nhut in South Vietnam, the 727 lifting away from the screaming and the green death, I worried that I would not make it. I worried that the plane would crash.

Far too quickly, because I remember that I did not even have time to dream, we were back in the world, 15,000 miles later, the sluggish plane circling above the fog off the cold bay.

I wanted to die then, even that newly removed from the implacable jungle. I wanted to die but I was too afraid, so I walked off that plane into the rain-misted California December morning and noticed first and most profoundly the absence of green.

I hadn't even known that I loved the green until that moment. It had been that overwhelming and holy green that I had first encountered a year before when I had landed in Vietnam. I noticed too how things smelled differently. Already I missed the musty jungle smell that had followed us everywhere, that reeked through our clothes and our gear.

You've got to keep your gear straight. You've got to keep your top knot tight and your utensils clean.

I want to tell you how the jungle makes its way inside you like a worm; how it finds itself a home there in the pink and warm of you where it grows. I want to tell you how the triple canopy of trees will not let proper light pass. I want to tell you about that light, but it hurts my eyes to remember. It is the light of bodies ascending through the heavy jungle air into the river of peace we wanted to believe lingered somewhere above us. It did not linger there, or anywhere. There was no peace. There is no peace for those torn wildly from the world.

That is all in the after. For me the after is rich with faith, or is faithless. It is drunk on the power of terror.

39

In the before my father came home late from the mill one cold Christmas Eve when I was nine or ten. He put some wrapped presents on the table and told me not to touch them. He told me exactly three times. I remember his shadow on the kitchen wall, and then he was out the door again, liquor on his lips when he kissed me roughly good-bye.

In the before my sister, who was older and should have known better, opened the boxes and left the gifts of perfume and hose my father had bought for his sisters and my mother scattered on the floor. My sister had imagined that they were something special for her, and when she saw that they weren't, she lost interest and vanished into her girl's life and then to bed. My mother was still at work in the meat locker; my father was out sharing some Christmas cheer after work.

In the before I am afraid to touch the presents. I want to wrap them up again so he will find them just as he left them and not come home angry, but I fall into the sleep of the deeply fearful. I press myself against the wall and imagine I am someone else, someone happy, my sister in the bed across from mine, the peaceful way she lingered there.

In the before she did not know that when he came in and found the scattered presents and torn wrapping paper that he dragged me out of bed. She didn't know how he jerked me by my arm against the wall. I was dreaming of snow. It was Christmas and snow blew wildly all around me when his belt flashed. He must have seen the blood and stopped, but in the dream the snake keeps striking. I hear the leather belt whip through the air behind him in the dark. In the before I waited in the dark for the belt to flash.

In the after, Christmas, 1967, I waited with my chums for the morning death toll after a night of rockets and mortars. For forty-nine consecutive nights we were hit by 122-millimeter rocket fire launched from the mountains around our base camp. After the first few had landed, we'd rush from our tents into a bunker nearby. Always they came in the dark morning hours, and sometimes I'd be back to sleep in the tent so quickly I would forget by dawn that the rockets had come again. During those forty-nine nights of rockets, I lost my sleep forever. Never again would I be able to find the kind of sleep I'd had in the before.

In the middle of these long weeks of barrage, a lovely young captain named Carter would die. He was tall and blond. At university he'd been an athlete. He was kind, and unlike most of the other officers, he liked us and spent time with us. He shared our dope those nights the rockets roared in. One dark morning when we'd scrambled to the bunker after being woken from our half-sleep by rockets, Captain Carter left the bunker to fetch his boots and helmet from the tent. It must have been just at the moment he entered that the tent took a direct hit from a rocket.

A 122-millimeter rocket is seventy-five inches long and carries one hundred pounds of explosives. This one had been so close to the bunker that we hadn't heard it come the way you heard the ones that pass. They sound like a train you might hear in your sleep, or like a storm in the dark. We didn't hear it come but we heard it hit, an explosion that shattered my hearing for weeks to come. By the time we got to him he was drowning in his own blood. He had one boot on and his eyes were so wide I wanted to close them. He'd taken a large piece of rocket shrapnel in his throat and the artery there was gushing. He was trying to cough up his own blood that was drowning him and that his whole body heaved against. The medic was too far away to help and the rockets still roared in around us. One boy with me in the bunker tried to press against the Captain's throat to make the bleeding stop, but the shirt he held there quickly soaked through with blood. I tried to hold Captain Carter down; he heaved so powerfully we were afraid he'd tear his heart out. We didn't know what to do. His eyes looked back and forth frantically at each of us, looking for an answer we didn't know. When his coughing and gurgling got loud and sounded like it came from deep in his chest, I suddenly put my mouth over his neck where the shrapnel had torn a hole. I hadn't thought about it. I found myself trying to suck the blood from his throat and lungs before I realized what I was doing. I remember that the other boys looked at me with such a great sadness that I thought they wanted me to stop. I know now that they knew it was too late and they were sad because they saw that I didn't know. I began to suck the blood out of the Captain's throat. I thought that if he could breathe again, he'd have a chance.

In the before, the injured and the beaten had always had a chance. In the after, Captain Carter died in our arms.

40

In the before some men's voices rose and fell far away. Time changed. Time got stupid and I stood in line with my brothers, our drawers at our feet so we could pull apart our cheeks. We were all there to get our physical before being sent to the Army. Some boys did not want to go. Some boys took pills or stayed up all night eating sugar to blow their blood pressure out of range.

Standing in line with our drawers at our feet so the doctors could look up our asses, I saw that one boy's hole was plastered closed with what looked to me like months of his own dried shit. The young doctor called a second doctor in. Word must have spread because soon some sergeants feigning aimlessness arrived

Oh la, the boy sang to the doctors, who giggled like men wh they dream about war. I could not imagine that a man would himself like that and let his own shit dry himself closed. I d know you could do that so they would not take you into the so they would not make you cross through the door of the greenery's mist. They took the boy away. They dra through the room and down a hall.

Oh la, he kept singing, until we couldn't hear him wondered what they would do to him. I didn't know had saved himself, that no matter what they did, it ter than the after.

All that night I rode out on a slow train with my cousin to Fort Knox and Basic Training. I could not stop thinking about the boy who had shit himself shut and I got drunk from whiskey we'd smuggled onboard. I drank so much that I pissed from the upper berth down onto my cousin passed out in the berth below. He never woke up so I thought I should wash him soapy-clean for the killing that I didn't know awaited us.

In the before I arrived at the clipped and crisp grounds of my Army Basic Training Company, Echo-18-5, at Fort Knox, Kentucky, on June 13, 1967, exactly seven days after I graduated from the Admiral Ernest J. King High School. Fort Knox was not the worst place to do duty. The base was not far from the bars of E-town and the women who would dance even with soldiers, and not far from the strip joints of Louisville we would stumble upon soon enough, in the drunken randomness of the weekend pass. This was in the before when we could still feel our own bodies.

I was eighteen years old. I was big and strong, six-feet-three-inches tall and one hundred seventy pounds. I was fit, and I knew already how to be gung ho; cruel coaches had already taught me that. I was used to playing hard and I loved contact, real contact. thought I was ready for anything.

The long first day began with all of us getting off the bus into un-streaked Kentucky morning, tanks from the armor units ing in the distance, early morning artillery practice booming. The bus had picked us up at dawn at the train station in Lou- . All night from Cleveland we had ridden the train, my first de ever, and I drank nearly two bottles of cheap whiskey cousin had smuggled onboard. He had come into the th me. He would follow me to the war after my first s there, where he would be wounded slightly.

Not long after the war I went to visit him in the house where he lived with his mother. We still couldn't say much. He offered me beer. He said he was looking for work. He offered me his cigarettes. He looked around his mother's living room nervously, as if he expected someone. We all expected someone, that's why we all still sit facing the door.

After a while he motioned for me to follow him upstairs to his room. He wanted to show me something, he said, and peeked around the corner to make sure his mother wasn't near. I thought he probably had some dirty pictures from R and R in Bangkok. He went to his closet. His room smelled of gunpowder and cheap cologne. On the walls were three gun racks. He pulled a brown paper sack from deep in the closet. He called me over to the closet's light, smiling. As I stood there awkwardly in that threshold with him, our shoulders touching, he opened the bag so I could see the brown and shrunken human ears that he'd cut off the bodies of VC. For many years I did not go back to his mother's house. I saw him sometimes in Lorain and we would greet and then pass like mere acquaintances.

When we got off the bus and stood in loose formation, the drill instructor greeted us with a sweetness that was so seductive I was not sure if it was real or some kind of sick joke. Even then I thought there was something dubious about the way he smiled, but I could not get around the easy way he seemed to care for me and put me at my ease, standing there among the others, the war for us only an unseen, bloody curtain.

I would come to feel that day the way I'd felt years before when we were wrenched by my father out of our 30th Street apartment and dropped down again on 17th Street, where I had been admitted into the generous company of others, into the 17th

Street Explorers club. Like back then, I felt a part of some force that moved as if on its own, but which I was somehow inside. I remember thinking of ants working around their hill. I knew I could be like the ants and this made me happy again. I belonged to something.

After a week of indoctrination, testing and then gathering our gear and uniforms together into duffel bags, we were assigned a permanent Basic Training barracks. My cousin and I would bunk together. He offered me the top. Our drill instructor, Sergeant Harden, told us we could bunk together in Basic, but that it would be the last time. When we went to Vietnam they'd have to split us up. "You can't have two family members standing in the same spot at the same time," the Sergeant said. "They don't mind if you die, they just don't want you to die together. That would not be fucking good."

He smiled when he said this the way he'd smiled at us when we'd first arrived. Weeks later I'd finally learn that this smile was not mocking, as it seemed, or devious or cruel, but rather the smile of someone who has seen too much to remember; a smile that comes from the irony of being alive after being among so many dead.

For a long time I did not trust Sergeant Harden. He could be wildly imaginative in his harassment of us, especially during those first few weeks of Basic. Once he had us fall out in the middle of a soaking midnight rain with our footlockers straddled on our shoulders, standing at attention.

He'd come among us quietly, slipping past the fireguard unseen. I know, because I saw him do it later, that he stood in the bay for a few minutes, watching us sleep, smiling in moonlight that came in through the bay windows. After a few minutes he walked down the entire length of the bay, rapping hard and loud on our metal bed frames with a short billy club he liked to carry.

"Rise and shine, girls," he said. "This ain't the world anymore. This ain't mommy time or girlfriend time or Coca-Cola time. You're on Army time now. Rise and shine," he said and smiled and then almost under his breath he said, "And fall out with footlockers."

I paused then. We had become accustomed to Sergeant Harden waking us up hours before reveille, taking us on short and intense forced marches through dark corners of the base no one recognized. But this was different. I paused because I wasn't sure he said what I thought he'd said.

In the before I was a squad leader. I'd been chosen for this privileged position because I'd screamed the loudest during our early days of exercise and sloppy formations. I never walked anywhere; I ran hard and always was the first to arrive. I'd spent too much time around single-minded, pathologically driven football and baseball coaches not to know how to please a drill instructor. I was perfect fodder. I had been trained in violence at an early age among my working-class family and my friends in Lorain. My advanced training had come at the hands of coaches, especially football coaches, from whom I'd learned how to love pain, mine and others.

When Sergeant Harden ordered us to fall out with footlockers that rain-soaked midnight the twelve soldiers in my squad asked me what he meant with their eyes. I didn't know, but there wasn't time to think about it, to figure it out. It was an order that we had to follow, without any questions, like all of the other orders in the before and in the after. I knew how to follow orders.

"Just fall out with your footlockers like the Sergeant said," I told them.

"How should we hold them?" one guy asked me.

"On your shoulder," I said, "how else?"

We stood out in the rain in our underwear and boots, our heavy footlockers balanced on one shoulder, some of us struggling to keep them there. Sergeant Harden waited a long time before coming out. I kept looking back over my shoulder towards the empty barracks where we'd left him. My squad squirmed and mumbled quiet complaints but I kept them in order and made them stand there without saying a word or making a sound. I wanted to be sure that my squad would not come into his disfavor, that my squad would stand out among the other three squads as the best in the platoon: the most upright and unmoving under the weight of their footlockers in the rain.

When he did come out, Sergeant Harden was smiling. He walked among the company of boys we were. He helped a few trainees reposition their footlockers for a better hold. He looked into our eyes, shaking his head yes and no in turn. He seemed genuinely pleased that we were there, that we'd followed what was obviously an absurd order by falling out in our underwear in the rain, humping footlockers on our shoulders.

We had not questioned command in the middle of the night and Sergeant Harden was happy because we had passed an important test in his mind. We had done something we did not understand, which had seemed mad or out of control if you stopped to think about it, simply because we had been ordered to do so. More than once in the months to come in the green place, I would come to see the beauty of this teaching. More than once it would save my life.

Sergeant Harden looked at me a long time that night in the before. More than once I thought he would say something to me but then seemed to change his mind. After he'd looked us over for a few minutes, he turned his back on us and began to walk out of the Company area into the darkness.

"He's fucking crazy," someone said under his breath. Another guy in my squad wanted to know what we were supposed to do then, but I didn't know.

I watched Sergeant Harden walk easily away from us until he was nearly out of earshot, and then I saw him stop and turn back towards us. He raised his head up slightly and I heard him say, almost too softly to be heard, "At ease," which meant that we could go back in the barracks and back to sleep.

41

Another time, later in the training cycle, I was leading my squad through some night maneuvers with the rest of the company. We'd been dropped off after dark in a stand of trees I'd never seen before and given a map with instructions on where to go and what our objective was.

The assistant drill sergeant told us that mock mines with tiny firecracker-like explosives would be in our path and that we had to find them without setting them off. Whoever set one off was dead, the sergeant said. He said that if you got dead you had to lie there until someone came along and told you otherwise. "You stay there just like you're dead," the sergeant said.

We were also told to expect contact with an enemy. Drill instructors from other companies from all over the Basic Training Brigade, dressed like the Vietcong in black pajamas, would be lying in ambush for us. We were to spot them before they had a chance to strike and to mock-fire our heavy M-14 rifles in their direction once we'd made contact.

I could see that some of my sweet, rough chums were uneasy about the whole enterprise, so I tried to show them my own exaggerated confidence. I was not confident, but I was not afraid either. I was excited. I relished the thought of playing war at night in the woods with the chance of real explosions going off and the chance that the VC would strike. I wanted to see them. I wanted contact. It was like a scrimmage to me, like some kind of drill we'd do in summer two-a-day football practices.

Almost immediately I got myself and my squad hopelessly lost in the dark woods. I'd led them off the path by following the coordinates we'd been given. Too late I realized a small mistake: a left turn instead of a right, west instead of east. I tried to lead them back to the path but we couldn't find it in the dark woods and instead came to a paved road. I told the squad to stay low and to crouch down on the edge of the road until I could check it out in both directions to make sure the way was clear. I was only a few feet from the road when I felt a force at my neck. I dropped my rifle and tried to escape the force but I was pulled down hard into the brambles, a powerful hand over my mouth and a knee in the center of my chest pinning me down.

"What in God's name are you doing, Weigl," Sergeant Harden asked me, and smiled down into my face. I was glad it was him and not one of those mock VC who would not have been as generous as my sergeant.

"I'm lost Sergeant," I said.

"No," he said, "you're worse than fucking lost. You're fucking dead and so is your squad."

"But we didn't have any contact, Sergeant," I argued, "and we hadn't tripped any of the mines."

"You're dead, Weigl, because you're in the middle of Indian country at night and you don't know where the fuck you are and you don't know what to do next except crouch in the weeds by the side of the road."

"What should I do, Sergeant?"

He reached down into the weedy ditch along the road and brought a handful of mud close to my face. "Rub this on your face," he said. "You don't have enough camouflage. I could see you guys from fifty meters. And don't make so much fucking noise. Tell those girls to keep their traps shut."

I did as I was told. I rubbed streaks of mud down my cheeks and across my forehead and Sergeant Harden smiled his sweet approval.

He let me stand up then and he brushed my fatigues off.

"Tonight you're lucky that your worst enemy is me. In Vietnam, I promise you, you will never have a second chance like this. No one will step forward out of the trees if you're lost to show you the fucking way. Before you even know what has happened, your throat will be slit open and you'll hear yourself die."

Sergeant Harden was not smiling as he said this, so I was afraid. I was suddenly afraid of being out in those woods among the VC drill instructors and their tiny mines, and for the first time, I was afraid of going to the war. Listening to my sergeant, whom I loved, his camouflaged face just inches from mine so I could see his sweat run down his face in tiny rivulets of greasepaint, looking at him that way, I shuddered through a fleeting moment of real terror at the thought of our war becoming real.

42

There was a before and then there was an after. There were many small befores, and one irrevocable after.

On June 6, 1967, I graduated into the humid, slag-heavy air from the Admiral Ernest J. King High School. My mother and my father were there. My Yugoslav grandmother Anna Grassa wanted her picture taken with me. My sister was there. I can hardly imagine them. I did not have a sense of the heaviness of their bodies.

Our valedictorian made a grand speech, primarily about his own accomplishments. No one liked him. My chums and I sat in the back and made noises with our hands that sounded like flatulence. In the small space between two names being called out over the public address system, we made cups with our hands and added other names, names that were jokes, like Manual Labor or Who Flung Poo. This was in the before when we believed that laughing out loud could save you from the hard facts of a wasted life.

After we got our diplomas, Pat, Rab, Bill, Hank and I headed out in Bill's car for some liquor to celebrate. We got this older guy who worked at the Slovenian Club to buy us bottles of cheap sweet wine in exchange for a fifth for himself. I swear to Christ we turned the heater of the car up as high as it would go and blasted the fan with all of the windows rolled up and drank that shit through straws until we were somehow even more stupid than before we had started drinking.

Before and After

With these boys who loved me first and best the way boys loved then, I spent my last six days of a life we had no way of knowing was being ripped terribly away from us. We dared our sweat-sheened bodies at each other. We slept together those last days before my departure and ate and drank together and took of each other's food and beer and wine. They were trying to bring me into some kind of circle, but I pulled away.

In the before, on the night before my departure, I drove restlessly down the back streets of Lorain that I had memorized as if there were a door that had been there all along that I could find now and slide through and escape into another life where the stars would not explode in my face.

Then I went back to my chums who did not dare say the brutally simple good-byes but drank hard with me and touched me in their drunkenness and in the after, months later, lives later, leeches and rot and words like a ball of steel in my mouth, I would lie with another boy in the razor grass, his stomach torn open and glistening in the light breaking through the canopies of green, and I would remember those boys of my last nights in the world, their grace undone now, and then I would lose them forever in a war's wind swirling and give myself to the dying boy who begged me, above the liftship blast, not to tell his mother that he had died this way.

43

In the before Sally had said *Please be good to me* when I left. When I pretended to leave. I wasn't gone. I didn't go anywhere. It doesn't feel as if I've arrived anywhere.

The rest of them said much of the same: *Take care. Take it easy.*

Take it any way you can get it, one uncle joked, and slapped me on my buttocks and winked and made a clacking noise with his tongue.

I can see them waving at the edges of my vision, but they're not clear. They could be calling me back. If I squeeze my eyes shut I can see them waving from the porch, then they walk back in the house. Across the damp lawn they walked and left me stranded until the bus would take me away.

There are portals through which other places may be entered. The Vietnamese know that. The Buddhists in Hue know that. Johnson didn't know it. McNamara, no. Nixon, not a clue. Those who fought and died in the green place knew it; those who'd managed to slip through one of those doors.

Some fall into the portals by mistake. Some see ghosts wherever they go, wherever they are. Some see animals where people sit. Lizards and snakes, sitting at the desks of businessmen. I have slipped in and out of more than one portal like that.

One day I was in Lorain, on a cold December morning, doing nothing. I was doing what I've always done best in my life: hanging out. I was not paying attention. I was not marking time or paying homage to the trees in the wind that tried to tell me something. I was just there, occupying a small space, courting nothing. I was the Michelangelo of waiting. The Galileo of hanging out. I chose not to move too quickly through the world in those days. I was not paying attention.

One day I was in Lorain and the next in the tropics, sweltering and amazed by the lushness. I remember waking from one way of seeing every detail of the world into another. One day in Lorain and the next day in the great corrupted Republic of our Vietnam. There are portals you may fall into.

I love my country like the opera star loves her deaf child. I'm the man who doesn't have anything, but I love my country.

In the before, we marched in tight formation with Sergeant Harden counting cadence and singing us through a song that was our good-bye song before we knew it. To sing that way, with that platoon of boys in the hot Kentucky night as we marched, was as close to glory as I had been. At night in the barracks I'd lie awake and watch my brothers sleep. I tried to match my breath with theirs. I tried to be like them in all ways, and they like me, and all of us like each other: how the many become the one in order to die more bravely. We marched in fine and smooth formation and sang our marching song:

> *Around her neck*
> *She wore a pair of jump boots*
> *She wore them in the springtime*
> *In the merry month of May*
>
> *And if you asked her*
> *Why the hell she wore them*

The Circle of Hanh

She wore them for her trooper
Who is far far away

In the before I asked a lot of questions. I thought about the song the Sergeant had taught us and had liked to lead us through as we marched. One night I sneaked back to the Sergeant's room in the back of the barracks. He came to the door in his underwear. He was drunk on whiskey and he swayed there, trying to focus his eyes on me.

"What do you want, Weigl," he said when my face became clear.

"I want to know what the song means," I said. "The song about the woman with the jump boots that we sing when we march. I want to know what's behind the words."

Sergeant Harden stared hard at me then and seemed to sober up and regard me differently than before, as if he thought I'd just had my first idea.

"You want to know what the song means because you think there is something behind the words? Do I have that straight, Weigl?"

"Yes, Sergeant. I want to know if the song means anything. If it means we're going to die."

"You're worrying about the wrong shit, Weigl, but I'll tell you what it means so you can go back to sleep."

He stepped back and we went into his room. He pointed to a chair for me to sit on and then sat back on his bed, picking up a coffee cup of whiskey. He took a long drink, wiped his mouth with the back of his hand and looked at me again, that maddening Sergeant Harden smile already forming on his lips.

"The woman wore a pair of boots around her neck because she loved the man so much," he said. "The man who was far away.

Before and After

The man who showed her photograph to his comrades in the dark. This is not some Jody-fuck story. She wore the boots around her neck, is what the song says, and there's nothing behind the words except the weight of the boots on her white neck."

He sang the rest of the marching song then:

> But in the back
> Her father kept a shotgun
> He kept it in the springtime
> In the merry month of May
> And if you asked him
> Why the hell he kept it
> He kept it for her trooper
> Who was far far away

In the before we hid in the dark trees from drill instructors dressed in black pajamas. We pretended we were in harm's way so that we might learn to survive.

In the after we saw flesh ripped in unimaginable ways from human bodies. In the after the VC dressed sometimes in black pajamas. We were in their country. We walked as if we were kings through their gardens and their rice.

44

In the before we had pretended to be dead in mock battle. In the after a boy named Albright set a dead VC up against a tree so it looked as if he was standing up. It looked like the VC was leaning against the tree and bent slightly forward at the waist. Albright arranged the dead VC's hands so that they rested near his crotch.

Then Albright went over to the other side of the tree so you couldn't see him, and he started pissing, facing out in the same direction as the dead VC, so it looked like the dead guy was pissing. Then Albright came back around and put the dead VC back into a sitting position, all of this without a word, or without changing the same stony expression on his face we all carried in those days.

In the before we played dead in mock battle. In the after Albright liked to fuck with the dead.

Everyone had his ticks, his odd habits brought more brutally to the surface in the war. Albright liked to commune with the dead. He would take care with them. He would straighten them up, pull down their sleeves that had been blown upwards by the blast of artillery or B-52 strikes. He would straighten their hats or helmets, wipe dirt and grit and blood from their faces. No one said a word to him about it, except the LT just out of ROTC who couldn't read a map and got himself and some others shot up in an ambush he should have seen coming. He told Albright to leave the dead alone. He told Albright that if he didn't stop, he'd have him court-martialed and sent to prison. This is not the right thing to say to someone in the middle of a war in a green place. To threaten someone in the middle of a green war is a reckless thing.

A few nights afterwards, the LT was seriously wounded in the ambush he walked into. He was medivaced to Hawaii and the rest of the platoon took it as an omen. Leave Albright alone. There was enough to worry about without fucking with someone else's karma. There was enough karma to worry about in the dark.

In the before I once found a nearly dried-up creek in the woods near my house in South Lorain. The only water left in the creek was a hole of water three feet deep and four feet around. It was thick and churning with twenty-inch carp that'd been trapped there as the creek had dried to this hole. I looked around because I must have known the wrong I was about to do. The carp slashed wildly when I stepped into the hole, but they had no escape from my frenzied taking of them all with my knife.

In the after, one late Tet afternoon we'd come upon twelve or fifteen North Vietnamese Army regulars huddled in death together in a banyan tree fall. The LT told the platoon to dig in nearby. Albright walked around to each dead soldier after they'd been cleaned of paper and weapons, speaking quietly to them, straightening their uniforms, tucking their shirts into their pants.

Without much fuss or worry, and in a gray zone he'd managed to find away from our care, he soaked the bandanna from his head with canteen water and washed their faces and hands. After an hour or so of this work, he looked up at the few of us watching.

"I'm getting them ready for the other side," he said, then he looked especially hard at me and said, "You'd better hope I'm around when you buy your lunch, pal; you'd better hope somebody is around your dead and sorry ass who knows what to do to get you ready, or you might just end up in some shit hole worse than this one."

He bent over to brush a bit of mud from a soldier's bloodied face, and then he turned to face me and the others, his arms raised high in the air like a preacher's.

"My theory of the universe," he said, "based upon my experience in this war, says that there are shit holes spread out all through the cosmos. There are wars raging out there right now in space that haven't even happened yet in our time, like stars being born and then exploding in on themselves. This is not a nice place to die, this so-called Republic of Vietnam, but there are worse places out there."

He stopped and pointed to the sky just turning towards evening, and then he went back to his work.

45

In the before, a 122-millimeter rocket once exploded so near me that it rattled my whole being. I felt my brain slam hard against the inside of my skull. The rocket killed our captain, who'd left the safety of the bunker to run into the tent for his boots, and although no shrapnel tore into me that morning, the force of the blast's concussion blew my eardrums out.

I kept feeling all over my body once I'd gotten back on my feet, because a strange numbness had come over me and I thought that I might have been dead. I felt all around my body in the dark bunker for blood, but there was no blood. I struggled to open my eyes as wide as I could as if to let the life back inside of me. I wasn't wounded, but I knew that something had happened, that something was wrong, that I was different than I'd been before the blast.

Once the rocket attack had ended and we made our way out of the bunker, I ran over to my sergeant and asked him how I looked. I asked him if I was all right. He looked at me as if I were crazy, or if he hadn't understood what I said, so I asked him again. His lips were moving, but I could not hear the words. He reached with his hand as if to touch my face. Afraid because I thought he would hit me, I pulled away. I looked around wildly, trying to understand what had happened. He reached for me again, and because there was some tenderness in his eyes, I let him touch me. He ran the fingers of one hand down the side of my head, from the tip of one ear to my jawbone, and then he held up his bloody fingers for me to see. He was saying something over and over. I could tell by the way his lips made the same shape that he was repeating whatever it was he wanted to tell me, but I couldn't hear. I ran my own fingers over both of my ears in the morning dark of Camp Evans, north of Hue on Highway One, as if I was trying to wipe some cobwebs away. When I pulled my fingers away from my face and held them close, I could see that they were covered with blood.

"What's wrong with me," I said.

I must have screamed the words because he covered his own ears then and held a finger up to his lips as if to shush me. He grabbed me by my arm and pulled me towards the tent we shared. Men were running in different directions all over the base camp. I felt the blast of a helicopter taking off nearby and looked up to see it so close above me that I ducked. I closed my eyes to keep the dust out, but I could not hear the rotors roar.

My sergeant pulled me into the tent and pushed me down on his bunk. He poured some water from a canteen onto the front of his green T-shirt and tried to rub the blood from my face. What made me most afraid was that I felt no pain. I had only this strange numbness all over my body, and the sense that the world was pulling away from me. I held on to him and asked again what was wrong with me.

"You're OK," he said. He said it slowly now, over and over, being careful to shape the words with his lips so I could read them in the dim light of the tent.

He touched my face again and mouthed the words "You're OK, Weigl. You are not hit."

I calmed down a bit then. I tried to talk but my jaw was stiffening already, and then I began to feel so dizzy that I had to lie down on the floor. He turned away when I did this and I saw him reach for something near his bunk. He turned back with a small notebook and a pencil.

Wait, I saw his lips say, and he held up one finger for me to wait. He wrote something quickly in the notebook and held it up close to my face for me to read.

You're not hit, the note said. *The blast from the rocket blew your eardrums out. The blood is from your ears,* the note said. *That's all. You'll be all right.*

I lay there for a long time on the floor inside the tent, my sergeant standing over me, saying things I couldn't hear. I closed my eyes finally. I felt as if I needed to grab on to the world because it felt like it was spinning away from me. I closed my eyes and in the roar of the not-hearing, I must have passed out, or maybe just fallen asleep, because I didn't remember anything more until I opened my eyes and saw that I was in the medic's tent, surrounded by wounded and dying soldiers. Because the doctors and medics in the tent must have quickly determined that my injuries were not life-threatening, they tended to the others for a long time before anyone came to me.

A medic finally came over and shined a light in my eyes. He asked me something that I couldn't hear or read on his lips, and when I pointed to my ears and shook my head no, he nodded as if he understood. I saw him reach for something then turn back to me on the cot, a spring-loaded morphine syringe in his right hand. I started to stop him. I wanted to tell him that I wasn't in any pain, I just wanted him to do something so I could hear again, but he pushed me gently back down on the cot and I felt the needle shoot the morphine into my hip.

Be still, he mouthed to me. *Don't move now.*

I did what I was told. I closed my eyes and felt the drug begin to make its way through my body. It felt like a snake inside of me, making its slow way from somewhere below my waist upwards until I felt it settle inside of my head, dulling the roar of the silence a bit. I wondered what had happened to the other men. In the mornings after rocket attacks at base camp, we'd always hear about who had died, and who'd been wounded. Slowly word would make its way across the sprawling base camp. Sometimes the dead were boys we knew and sometimes not, but always my first thought was I was glad it hadn't been me.

I said that to myself as the morphine began to take me into a warm and drowsy half-sleep that I gave in to. I tried to say the words, *I'm glad it wasn't me,* but my lips would not move and no sound came, and then I stopped trying to speak. I stopped trying to think, or to be anything. I wanted only to go home then. I wanted to see my mother and my father. I wanted to tell them that even if I'd never hear again, it was okay. I wanted to know that they could still love me as they did before.

46

I came back from the after into the before, but it wasn't there anymore. Into the cold Ohio December, I came back to try to live among my people. I was afraid of something that I didn't have a name for. Beginning from that first moment in December 1967, and extending so far out into my life and into the lives of others that it is impossible for me to say where it ended, if it ever did, was a slow unraveling, a spiraling into more than one kind of hell.

I didn't know then that love could save me. I felt wholly unworthy of any human kindness, not because of anything I'd done in the war, but because of what I'd seen. I was filled with a vague doubt and an incomprehensible guilt that made me feel like I was drowning. To hide this grief from my family, I became someone else for them, and although it seemed at times that I could find my way back into the life I'd left behind only a year earlier, I was nagged by a vague suspicion that they could tell something wasn't right. I'd catch my mother or father watching me out of the corner of their eyes as if they expected me to suddenly jump up from the sofa in their living room and do something that would bring terror into their lives.

Before and After

I couldn't sleep that first month home. I sensed that something or someone was waiting for me in the dark to drop my guard, and that if I allowed myself to fall asleep, it would come and find me, and make me pay for the horror I could not have avoided bringing with me from the war.

I'd pretend to go to sleep like the others in my mother and father's house, not unlike the way I pretended to go to sleep those nights with Sharon when I knew she'd come and get me as soon as my sister had gotten quiet in her own bed. When I thought my mother and father had gone to sleep I'd get up quietly and go into their living room with a blanket and a pillow. I'd watch the three channels on their television until the anthem played and the test pattern came on and then I'd sit up that way, alone, until I could see some daylight gathering in the trees and then I'd slip quietly into my bedroom and finally allow myself to fall asleep.

I didn't know then that love could save me. I believed that I was beyond the forgiveness of the good people around me. I thought that drugs would save me.

I'd starting smoking grass in Vietnam, and when I came home, I discovered that my friends who'd stayed behind had also started smoking. In the war we got high almost every day. It became part of who we were, allowing us to go through the motions of soldiering in an army out of control, in a war that no one believed in anymore. After I'd been home for a few weeks, I figured out where I could get what I needed. I took whatever was offered and let the drugs have their way with me. Either because I didn't think I could ever die, or because I believed I was already dead, I wasn't afraid. I liked the way my excesses amused my friends, who, I came to understand, knew nothing about risk or about danger. They thought they were taking chances by trying drugs; they thought they were risking something, but I believed then that they didn't have a clue because they hadn't seen what I had seen.

I thought that women could save me then. Women either came to me easily and offered themselves, or I schemed and acted out some dubious plot in bars or lonely bedrooms so that I might hide under the wings of what I imagined was love. I took what I could get and wanted more. Waking up naked in a stranger's bed after a night of drugs and drinking, I would sometimes have only a vague memory of how I'd ended up there, or what I'd had to do to stay. I thought that fucking as many women as I could would save me, that as long as I was giving someone what sounded and looked like pleasure, whatever it was that was waiting for me in the dark would be kept at bay. I still needed to keep the dragons at the gate those nights. I know now that I had an almost uncontrollable need to put my life in jeopardy, and to live as if the only thing that mattered was feeling, as intensely as I could, my body and my heart. Drugs let me feel that way, and sleeping with women I didn't know, who must have been drawn too to the danger, made me feel that way as well.

Some nights, as we lay in bed together, a woman I'd met at a bar that day, or at the supermarket, would ask me about the war. She would imagine that she wanted to know more than the television had told her about what had really gone on, but I was at least aware enough to know that she didn't want to know. Sometimes a woman would ask if I'd killed anyone, and I would be overcome with an irresistible urge to get out. I'd lie, saying I was sick and needed to leave. I'd stand up suddenly and begin to dress myself in the dark. Sometimes she would ask me please to stay, that she was sorry, she understood if I didn't want to talk about it, but she wouldn't understand. The women thought they wanted to be close to what they imagined was danger, but I knew they didn't want what I had to offer.

I found myself squatted down one night on a curb in a frozen twilight parking lot some fucking where. I remember feeling as if I'd just woken from a bad and lonely dream, although this was not a new feeling, and I knew it wouldn't be my last night-terror.

I had come to know that it was only the old journeying again that I'd done all my life; that walking in and out of doors, crossing back and forth through portals that hold back the machine of time. When you pass back and forth so easily between worlds, you may see the fresh underbelly of things, and how the righteous and the wretched are one. Sometimes what is revealed fills me with horror and with dread.

That cold night I found myself in a city I couldn't name, looking up into the near apartment's windows and at the lives going on behind them in the light. I looked down at my hands and saw that the fingers of my gloves had holes. My coat was shabby and torn where the lapels had been and my shoes were too small so that someone, maybe me, had cut out the toes, through which my own toes protruded.

I don't know what I was doing there. There had been a war and my people had grown disenchanted. In my pocket I had a fifth of somebody's cheap whiskey. The whiskey kept me warm that night. For a long time I watched people move through the rooms of their apartments, and I tried to imagine the lives that lived there until I became a night wing in summer sky. I fluttered outside their windows, lit with a thousand watts of something I could taste and feel but could never name. I became the watcher in the dark again, stalking something I could not name then but that I know now was the story of my life.

47

I lived in that zone between being and not being for a long time. I think I must still live there now, only now there is no before and no after. There is only the story. Words make up what a life becomes whether we like it or not. We live most fully among the words, and in the words I found salvation.

Through the books other people led me to, through the stories I began to read and hear in a way that made me see the life in them, I was led back to my own life, and to the great chain of stories that had been inside of me all along.

As if by a river we are all connected by words. We need words to eat and to drink. We need words to wash away the ugly reality that we sometimes allow ourselves to imagine is a life, and we need the dirt and grit of our struggle in order to hang on to the spinning green planet that is our only home, that is inside of us like a story.

When I woke up from the long and drowsy years of no imaginings after the war, I woke up among words. Like my grandfather with a bowed piece of lumber, I tried to bend and shape words into what I imagined were useful things, stories that could be like a spar thrown to you when you're drowning.

The work of making those stories led me away from the world of hurt; it led me to the love of a good woman who is my long-time friend and my wife of the decades; my wife of the ocean night grass and of the milk-heavy mother breasts drowsily dipping towards me. My wife, my rope, my bread. Into the circle of her arms where love was calm as a pond, I was led by the story's grace; there I was allowed to bear witness to the stories that had made me who and what I was.

The work of making those stories led me back to the power of family, which is the place of stories, the source of the fire. It led me to the life of my son whom we brought among us so he could live with us inside the story of who we were, and then be blessed by words, but the work of such making is hard and dangerously easy to get wrong.

In my clumsiness to love most fully, and in my laziness before the difficulties of parenting, I let us fall into days and nights of such hurtful and desperate trouble that I imagined our only relief could be to kill us all.

Almost too late I came to realize that I didn't know what had gone on inside my son. I felt as if there were things, even in his boy's life, that he could not forgive himself for doing, or saying, or feeling. I saw him more than once, already as big as a man, curled up tightly into himself on the floor, crying and gagging on words that would not come to his lips, and I saw him more than once make people around him sit up and take notice of the gift of himself that he offers so sweetly I can hardly bear to imagine it. Only the story had the power to bring us back from that brink.

In the story of my son he steps back from the life he allowed to blur so that he could not see what to do. He steps back to see the need to take care with his life, and the need to love himself more fully and more deeply.

In my story he becomes the boy I know is inside of him who is good and strong, and who can endure the tumbling into the hurt of knowing.

When my son was a tiny baby, I walked one early sleepless morning, in those hours that used to be the hours of ambush, into his bedroom, looked at him sleeping and thought that he was more beautiful than the light before the light had touched anything. I didn't know what that light I saw when I looked down into his crib meant. I think now that it must have been the light of who he is already burning through.

In my story he remembers that he has that light inside him. He lets it come through and fill the room. He lets it lift him out of the darkness that wants to eat him because that's what the darkness wants: the darkness of self-hate, or the darkness of the place of no words. His is such a strong light that it lifts him away. It shines on him and helps him be the boy that he is, full of light. In the story of my son, there is no ending, only this beginning filled with light that is the story of light.

One of the things my son feared in those days was the adoption of his sister from Vietnam. Although he had been part of the process from the start, and had shared in our joy with her coming, he was also afraid that there would be less of us for him. He told me later that he knew he could never compete with an eight-year-old Vietnamese sister. For a while that fear pushed him away from us, and from himself. But the grace he has brought him eventually to the grace he saw in her life, once she had come among us and so bravely taken her place in our family.

It was something precisely like her gentleness that he needed. Her gentleness brought that part of him to the light again.

Part Eight

The Circle

of Hanh

48

Once we had landed in Hanoi, I felt so near Nguyen Thi Hanh that I thought I could smell her, and hear her voice.

Although my seat was near the front of the plane, I was exhausted, and waited until everyone else had exited before I got up to exit. It was November and already the air was becoming too cool for most Vietnamese, who wore sweaters or jackets. Still, it felt warm to me. I'd left central Pennsylvania in an early snowstorm and for weeks the temperature had been in the thirties at home.

Autumn in the northern provinces of Vietnam is an odd combination of high humidity and lowering temperatures. I felt too warm but I'd learned from previous trips to resist the temptation to wear summer clothing in autumn. When my Vietnamese friends saw me dress in summer clothes in the fall, they would always warn me that I was inviting sickness. The cool winds from China, they said, brought sickness, so although I was already sweating, I kept my jacket on as I walked across the tarmac to the terminal.

The airport was busy and those passengers who had deplaned before me had already formed long lines at each of the three immigration checkpoints. I wanted the time to think more about how to handle the visa problem. I was hopeful that the man whose name I'd been given in Hong Kong would be there to help me, and I took the time to look around the airport, beyond the restricted area where incoming passengers were processed, for any sign of my Vietnamese friends. I wasn't sure if my message about the visa had reached them.

As I reached the small booth and handed my passport and declaration papers to the immigration officer, I spotted Lady Borton and Nguyen Quang Thieu. They smiled and waved. They were still too far away to hear me so I shrugged my shoulders and held out my hands, palms up, in the universal sign that asks a question. In response Thieu gave me the thumbs-up and pointed towards the rear offices where the immigration officials were. I could read his lips when he mouthed the words *Duat is there. Duat is there*, pointing to the offices and smiling confidently.

He was referring to Pham Tien Duat, one of Vietnam's most beloved poets, with whom I'd become very close on my visits to Hanoi and during his visit to the U.S. Like most of Vietnam's popular writers, Duat was also well connected and seemed to have significant and broad influence in official matters. Duat is a beautiful man who never lost his boyishness in spite of the long years he'd spent on the Ho Chi Minh Trail during the American war. Knowing that Duat was already working on my case gave me renewed confidence.

It's difficult for most Americans to understand the high regard the Vietnamese have for poetry. For anyone growing up in Vietnam, hearing, reading, singing or writing poetry in either the written or oral tradition is as natural as breathing, and nearly as essential. This is true if one comes from the north, the highlands or the south, whether one is the child of teachers, farmers, soldiers, politicians, shopkeepers or musicians. Making poetry in one form or another is a widely accepted, expected response to the universal experiences of love, loneliness and separation.

When I travel to other universities to read from my poetry and from my translations of Vietnamese poetry, or when I talk to my own students about the place of poetry in Vietnam, I tell two stories to illustrate its importance in the culture.

During the American war, General Giap—who had helped defeat the French at Dien Bien Phu and, later, led the North Vietnamese Army against the Americans—had assigned Duat, a soldier for over ten years, the task of writing and reading poems for North Vietnamese Army soldiers as they traveled up and down the Ho Chi Minh Trail. To inspire them in their long struggle and to help them endure the enormous hardships of battle, the North Vietnamese Army relied upon poetry.

I can't speak for other American military outfits, but the 1st Air Cavalry, the division that I served with during my year in the war, did not have a designated poet. We had *Playboy* and USO shows that featured starlets with bad voices, flashing cleavage and dancing in miniskirts.

I also like to talk about how it is to be with Duat or any number of other well-known writers who have become my friends in the North. Walking through Hanoi with Duat, or eating with him at a street-side restaurant, is like walking through New York might be with Madonna or Michael Jordan: people come out of their shops to greet Duat and shake his hand, or just to say hello and remember to him one of his poems that they've memorized.

Sometimes, when I'm eating in a restaurant with Duat and other writers, it becomes necessary for the owner to put up a partition around our table to keep people away. It's not an unfriendly gesture, but a practical one. Duat is so popular and so generous when his readers approach him, that he might fail to finish a meal if he weren't given this privacy.

These are the things I thought about as I waited for the immigration officer to look over my passport and other papers. I was happy that I'd made it to Hanoi, and I was convinced that now that

I was there, I'd be able to resolve the visa problem with Duat's help.

The immigration officer looked at me for a long time without smiling then looked back down at my passport. He passed my papers back to me through the small opening in the glass front of his booth and in Vietnamese he told me that my papers were no good, that I could not enter Vietnam. I felt that same rush of sick panic that I'd felt in Hong Kong. I tried to speak to him in Vietnamese, but I was nervous and not paying enough attention to the tones. I could tell I wasn't making any sense. I asked for the man whose name I'd been given in Hong Kong, and I told him that Pham Tien Duat, my friend, was just now speaking to immigration authorities in the offices behind the booth. I pointed to where Lady Borton stood, now joined by Thieu.

I could tell by the look on his face that this sounded like a dubious story to him. I knew too that his instructions were clear. You either had a valid visa or you didn't. You could either enter Vietnam legally, or not at all. There was no room for reasoning or argument in his protocol. He pointed again to the dates on my visa and said, *"Khong tot,"* not good. I tried to tell him in Vietnamese that I knew the dates were wrong, but that they'd made a mistake at the Vietnamese embassy in the U.S. He told me in Vietnamese that he didn't understand what I was saying. He told me to step to one side so that others might have their papers processed.

After I'd sweat through a few more hot minutes, a man who appeared to be a higher-ranking immigration officer came to the booth, accompanied by Duat. They both spoke to the officer processing the papers and he asked me for my passport again. He passed it to the man with Duat, who quickly read it then shook his head no and made a tsking sound. Duat said something to him that I couldn't understand. The three of them went back and forth for another five minutes until I was finally allowed to pass through the gate into the open area of the airport. I breathed deeply and felt the panic pass again.

On the other side of the gate, Duat and I were joined by Lady Borton and Thieu. Duat's English was still rudimentary, like my Vietnamese, so Thieu and Lady Borton interpreted.

"The problem with the visa is a serious one," Duat said, and paused to allow Thieu to interpret. Although I'd been with Duat in more than one trying situation, I didn't remember ever seeing such dark seriousness on his face before, and all of the worries rushed back into my brain.

But, he added, holding up one finger to his lips, he was sure that we could resolve the problem, and that it was only a matter of reaching the right people to OK a new visa. In the meantime, because I was accompanied by Duat and Thieu, I was being permitted to sit in a waiting area in the unsecured part of the airport. He pointed to an area just outside a small airport shop that had some tables and chairs. He said we could sit there, drink some beer, smoke and talk while we waited.

"It's very serious," he said again, and stood on his toes to look directly into my eyes. He grabbed me by my arms, shook me a few times and said he thought it could be fixed. As we made our way to the table and chairs, Duat and Thieu spoke too quickly for me to understand. I walked beside Lady who told me they'd gotten my message from Hong Kong and had been working on the problem ever since, but there seemed to be some kind of snag somewhere. I sensed there was something she wasn't telling me, and saw in her the same seriousness I'd seen in Duat. Lady chided me for not being more careful about the visa. I wanted to explain to her how suddenly things had happened, how much I'd had to do to get ready to come, how the visa had arrived only on the morning of my departure, but I didn't. I told her I knew she was right (because she was right), but it was a knowledge that I could feel like a sharp, grinding thing in my gut.

We sat down while Duat disappeared into the small shop. Thieu told me he was happy to see me and asked me for pictures of Hanh. He held each one for a long time, smiling, before he passed them to Lady.

"She looks very smart in her eyes," he said. "You are very lucky."

I told him and Lady about the schedule and how important it was that I stuck to the itinerary provided by the adoption agency. I told them that everything depended upon my being able to get into Hanoi as soon as possible so I could prepare for the drive to Binh Luc the next day where the orphanage and provincial officials would be gathered.

"It's OK," he said. "Duat can help."

Duat arrived with beer for us all. He sat down at the table and after looking at the pictures of Hanh, he stood up again to offer a toast in her honor and in mine. His presence in this situation soothed me and I felt the sharp grinding thing that was my ultimate fear, that I'd have to leave Vietnam without Hanh, recede a bit.

Duat suggested that I invite a few of the immigration guards standing nearby over to join us. I waved to them, pointed at the empty chairs and held up a bottle of beer. They both smiled shyly and came over. Duat introduced me and they sat down to join us. Duat told them in Vietnamese that I was a famous American poet and a longtime friend to Vietnam. He told them I had come to pick up my daughter whom I was adopting from Binh Luc. They looked at the pictures together and smiled. One of the guards said something to me in Vietnamese that I couldn't understand, so Lady interpreted, "He said you are a very good man to do that, to bring Hanh into your home, and that you must love the Vietnamese very much."

I tried to respond in Vietnamese that I did love Vietnam but I immediately realized I'd used the wrong form of the word *love* that made everyone laugh. I had spoken about Vietnam as if the country were my lover. The guard needed interpretation. My accent was still very rough at times and though most of my Vietnamese friends could understand what I said, there were others who would look at me as if I'd just uttered the most unintelligible thing they'd ever heard. The two guards drank beer with us, smoked some cigarettes I offered and, after shaking hands with Duat, returned to their posts.

For nearly two hours we sat there. Every ten minutes or so Duat would disappear into one of the offices for five or ten minutes or walk over to a desk occupied by an immigration officer and use the phone. Twice he returned with different immigration officials, introduced me the way he'd introduced me to the guards and showed them the pictures of Hanh. I was beginning to fret again. I could feel the thing inside me start to turn slowly, like a jagged drill bit gouging deep in my body. When the pain began to radiate to my back I realized I hadn't been paying careful enough attention. The pain was suddenly familiar.

Twice recently—once in August when I had been fly-fishing for brown trout on the Little Juniata River with my friend Harry Humes, and once in late September as I had stood before an undergraduate poetry-writing class—I had to be taken to the hospital for kidney stones. I should have seen this one coming. I should have known that what I'd been feeling as far back as JFK Airport almost forty-eight hours earlier had been more than my anxiety about the trip or the visa problems.

I didn't know what to do. On top of everything else, I could hardly believe that this was happening to me. I was embarrassed to tell anyone. I began to drink enormous amounts of water, telling Duat and Lady when they asked that I was just a bit dehydrated. Lady said I looked a little pale and asked if I was all right. I told her I was just tired and anxious to get into Hanoi. Duat stood up to leave again and said something to Thieu that I didn't understand.

"Duat said he was going to the office of the head of the airport," Thieu said before I could ask. He said that Duat had spoken to the man on the phone when I had first arrived. The director had been in Hanoi most of the day but was due back any minute.

I tried to block the kidney pain that grew sharper and more consuming in measurable increments. I drank and pissed and drank some more. I did several silent meditations to try to keep the pain from taking me over and managed to dull it a bit. In the back of my mind I knew things would get worse before they got better. In the hospital at home they'd given me intravenous morphine both times I'd checked in with a stone and both times it took more morphine than even the doctors thought possible to ease the pain so I could bear it. Both times I'd eventually passed a piece of the stone but only after hours of deep, serious pain. I wondered what they could do for me here. I wondered if they'd take me to the hospital if I told them what was wrong, or if they'd think it was a ruse to get myself into the country.

Duat came back to the table accompanied this time by a man in a suit. I stood up and Duat introduced the man to me as the Director of the Airport. The Director was clearly not amused by my difficulties, but he shook my hand and joined us at the table. He looked directly at me and began to speak in slow and careful Vietnamese, with Lady Borton interpreting.

He said that the problem with my visa was very serious, and that I was in violation of Vietnamese law by being in the country without a proper visa. He said only the presence of my good friends had allowed me to clear the security guard in the first place. Those friends, he said, were in the process of trying to get me a new visa. He turned to Duat, said a few more quick things I couldn't understand, shook my hand and then walked away.

Duat spoke to Thieu and to Lady. I felt sick and dizzy. Duat talked to Thieu and Lady for a long time, and although I interrupted more than once to ask what he was saying, Lady told me to wait. Lady and Thieu looked grim and nodded their understanding as Duat spoke to them.

Finally, Duat turned to me. In English, he said, "This is a very serious problem. I have bad news." He paused and shifted to Vietnamese, asking Lady to interpret. "Even before you arrived in Vietnam from Hong Kong, a decision had already been made that you would have to leave on the next plane to anywhere outside of Vietnam. That is the law. Officially, your visa is expired and you cannot get a visa here at the airport simply by asking for one."

He shook his head and held my hands on the table.

"You have many friends in Hanoi," he said, "and we were able to convince the Director of the Airport to let you stay tonight so that the Writers' Association can secure your visa tomorrow. It's too late today. Everyone has gone home. Even the Director has cooperated. He'll have to lie to those in higher authority and say there was not an open flight for you to take tonight even though there were at least two or three. We convinced him by telling him about your work in Vietnam."

Duat pulled out a copy of the book of poems written by North Vietnamese soldiers that I had cotranslated from the Vietnamese.

"I showed the Director this book," Duat said, "and he agreed to help us." Duat stopped and shook his head again.

I waited for him to continue. I waited for the bad news, but that was the bad news, as it turned out. I would be allowed to stay in the Noi Ba Hotel across from the airport tonight. I would not be allowed to leave the grounds of the hotel until Duat and Thieu arrived the next morning with my visa. Thieu promised that they would go to work on the problem at 7 A.M. the next morning and said that they should have the visa by noon. I felt some relief. When Duat had spoken of bad news I was sure he meant I'd have to leave Hanoi immediately. To me, this news represented only a minor delay and although it would force me to reschedule my trip to Binh Luc, at least I was not being forced to leave the country, which would cause a chain of changes that would jeopardize the entire adoption. I could still conjure the clear image of Nguyen Thi Hanh at the end, waiting for me.

I smiled at Duat and told him not to worry. I told him I didn't mind staying in the Noi Ba Hotel for one night and I thanked him for his long hours of negotiation, and for his friendship. He hugged me and smiled. I remember now that I had forced myself at the time to deny something I saw in his eyes when he let go of the hug and backed away from me: a sadness that betrayed the smile. For a moment I felt a frightening instability so powerful that it came in the form of a physical sensation: I thought I felt the floor drop out from under me. As quickly as that sensation came, I tried hard to let it go. I had to believe.

Accompanied by an immigration officer, Duat, Thieu and Lady Borton walked me to the Noi Ba Hotel, directly across the street from the airport. It was a pleasant enough place, although something nagged at me even as we walked into the small lobby: some foreboding I couldn't quite find the source of seemed to linger in the air. I was exhausted and my body ached from the kidney stone I knew I'd have to contend with next. Duat approached the desk and exchanged small talk with the woman who passed me a key and a registration card to sign. On the card was a place to write my name, the sponsoring organization or ministry in Vietnam, my address, the purpose of my visit and the number of my passport and visa. The two spaces for passport and visa numbers had been crossed out by hand. When you stay at the Noi Ba Hotel, you have no passport or visa because your passport has been confiscated at the airport.

I had the sudden and dreadful recognition that I was on a long list of many who had come into country like me, without a proper visa, or without a visa at all, who had been sent away immediately, or sent to the Noi Ba Hotel until the next available flight out of Vietnam. I filled out the card and turned back to my friends. Again Duat and Thieu shook my hand and hugged me. I began to ask them if they would stay for dinner but before I finished, Lady interrupted and said that they weren't allowed to stay.

"Don't worry," she added quickly when she saw the dread come into my face, "they'll take care of it. It's only one night," she said. "You need the rest now anyway."

She was right, of course. I needed the rest and the time to deal with the sharp, calcified piece of misery that was ripping its way through my body.

"You're right," I said, and thanked them all again. I watched them walk through the lobby and out the door. I could still see them as they crossed the street into the airport parking lot. Already too far away for me to see his face, Thieu turned back and waved in the direction of the hotel. I knew he couldn't see me but I waved back. It was dark by now and the traffic noise of a million motorcycles was beginning to fade. I could hear the engine of a plane revving for takeoff, and then another.

49

A small boy grabbed my biggest suitcase, which I'm sure weighed more than he did, and began to lug it up the stairs, motioning with his eyes for me to follow. I caught up with him, took the heavy bag off his shoulder and handed him the two lighter bags. He laughed when I did this, touched the bicep of my right arm, made a sweet, mocking face of wonder and surprise and said, "OK."

Inside the room he put the bags down, turned the lights and air conditioner on and showed me a small refrigerator in the corner filled with bottled water, beer and Coca-Cola. He said something in Vietnamese that I didn't understand, which I told him in Vietnamese. He said it again slowly and I realized that he was asking me if I wanted something to eat. I told him that I did but that first I had to rest. I was thinking about the stone, my first priority, and about trying to call home and reach some friends who could call the Vietnamese embassy in Washington to ask for help in case things didn't work out in Hanoi. He said OK again and thanked me when I tipped him.

I immediately began to drink the bottled water from the refrigerator. I knew my only chance would be to wash the stone out of my system. Twice before I had failed at this task, even with the help of morphine and intravenous fluids, but tonight my options were limited. Within the next twenty minutes I drank all four one-liter bottles of water as well as a Coke. I felt a painful, hopeful urge to pass the water after another ten minutes and went into the bathroom. I looked into the bowl to see how clear the water was. I had to know if I could see the stone if it passed. The bowl was stained dark brown at the bottom and around the edges, and there were small pieces of something at the bottom that could easily pass for a stone so I flushed the toilet. I spread out two tissues and tried to use them as a screen. I pissed long and hard and although the stone did not come, I felt it move. The pain in my back eased a bit but almost immediately a new pain shot up in my groin.

I went back into the room and picked up the phone. The woman who had checked me in answered and I asked her for more water. She sent up the boy who'd carried my bags. He looked perplexed when I let him in. He pointed to the refrigerator and told me the water was there. I gathered and then held up the four empty bottles and told him I needed more. His eyes got big and he laughed and he said something in Vietnamese.

"*Hon nuoc,*" I told him, more water. He left and came back with four more bottles.

"*Khong lang,*" he said, not cold.

I told him it was OK and offered another tip, which he refused. After he had gone I started in on the next bottle, and then the next. After once again pissing through the tissue without success, I lay across the bed to rest for a few minutes before calling home. It was midnight in Vietnam, which meant it was 11 A.M. of the previous day back home. I thought for a moment about what day it was and then tried to remember my wife's schedule, but before I could calculate the best time to call, I fell asleep.

Suddenly, I sat up in bed. The kidney stone was digging in now, sending truly unbearable pain down into my scrotum. I thought I must have dozed for a minute or two. I went to the refrigerator and began to drink another bottle of water. In the dark room lit only by the small bulb of the refrigerator, I saw on my watch that it was 4 A.M. I could hardly believe I had slept four hours. I didn't feel rested at all. I wanted to call home but knew I should concentrate on hydrating myself as thoroughly as possible. After I finished two more bottles of water the pain was forcing me to moan out loud. I was embarrassed in an odd way. I didn't know what I would say to anyone, what I could possibly do. I knew from the other two stones that if this one didn't pass, nothing short of heavy morphine could help me. By this time I was delirious. Sitting upright, I rocked back and forth on the bed, pressing my right fist down hard just above my bladder and then squeezing even harder in a downward motion. There is no possible position that you can assume to ease such pain, a fact that only those who have suffered kidney stones can fully appreciate. I felt stupid. I had fucked up with the visa, I told myself, and now this stupid fucking kidney stone was somehow my reward.

By 4:30 A.M. I'd finished off the water, three Cokes and three bottles of beer but I couldn't seem to budge the stone and the pain had already taken me to the point where I knew it could be no worse. I stood up and walked around the room, pressing in on my bladder and pissing from time to time. There were only two bottles of beer left now and it was too late, or too early, to call for more water. At least the beer might give me some relief from the pain, I thought, and quickly drank another bottle and a half. I lay back down for a minute until a consuming nausea came over me, and before I could make it to the toilet, I vomited three times. I was burning up, soaked with sweat and my bladder felt shredded. After I'd emptied my stomach, I reached for another beer and gulped down half of it. I stood up, intending to go into the bathroom and wash up but the nausea came again so I sat back down. Again I

vomited violently. I moaned louder now. I think I hoped that someone would hear me. I hoped that someone would come and see
how bad off I was and take me away for help. I felt a deep physical
and emotional need to be cared for. I cried out loud and wished
I'd never come to Vietnam, that I'd never fought in the war or
returned, that I'd never thought about adopting a Vietnamese
child.

50

No one came, and just as I reached the threshold of doing something drastic to get help, I felt a sharp new pain, then almost immediately, some relief. I was wary, though. I could hardly believe that the pain was lessening, but when I stood up, it became
clear that something had happened. I drank the rest of the last
bottle of beer and went into the bathroom. Although I felt a very
strong urge to pass water, nothing would come. I strained against
my own body until I heard a small trickle fall into the bowl. I
pushed harder as I imagine women must push as the baby breaks
through. The trickle became a stream that increased as if on its
own. Just as I finished, I felt another sharp, burning pain. I realized that the burning was in my penis and just as I opened my
eyes to look down, I saw the small stone plop out with the last
few drops of urine.

Almost immediately I was revived. I felt my body celebrate the expulsion of the stone as if it were suddenly coming alive again. I reached down into the bowl to make sure. The size of my smallest fingernail, with sharp jagged ridges all around its circumference, it was the biggest stone I'd passed. I wrapped it in a piece of tissue, washed my face, brushed my teeth and walked out to find my watch. It was 6 A.M. In an hour Thieu and Duat would begin their efforts to get a new visa for me. I thought for a moment that I'd try to call home, then changed my mind. I needed to rest. If things went as I hoped, I'd have my visa by noon and soon after I would be on my way to Binh Luc, only a few hours behind schedule. I lay back down on the bed, savoring the kind of happiness that comes only when some great burden has been lifted from your body or from your heart. I blessed out loud the passing of the stone and immediately fell asleep.

The phone woke me at 7:30 A.M. I picked up the receiver to hear Lady's voice. She sounded cheerful and said she'd already spoken to Thieu and that she thought everything would be all right, that they'd have my visa by noon. I closed my eyes and thought of Jean and Andrew and of Hanh. I missed my wife and son suddenly. I wanted all of us to be together more than anything. Lady told me to rest, and promised to keep me posted. I fell off to sleep again and woke to someone knocking hard on my door. It was 8 A.M. and I wondered if they could have possibly gotten the visa and driven out to the hotel so quickly. I pulled my pants on and opened the door to an immigration officer and a man who introduced himself to me in English as the manager of the Noi Ba Hotel. The manager matter-of-factly explained that I had to pack my suitcase and leave immediately for a flight to Singapore that would depart at 8:30 A.M.

I didn't panic; I'd been through too much in the last twenty-four hours. Almost instinctively I began to stall. When my stalling became obvious, the immigration officer said something to the hotel manager that I didn't understand but that I knew was more bad news.

"You must hurry," the manager said. "This man is responsible for making sure you're on the flight to Singapore. You are in violation of Vietnamese law and you can no longer stay in the country."

I began to explain my situation regarding the visa. He recognized Duat's name when I told him that Duat was working on getting me a new visa as we spoke. The manager interpreted for the guard who listened but grew more and more impatient and worried. I knew it wasn't personal. I knew he could jeopardize his position if he didn't follow the order he'd been given. He looked at me with disbelief and told me that I had to leave immediately. The manager interpreted but I told him in Vietnamese that I'd understood.

"Quickly, please sir, quickly," the manager said and began to help me get my things together. I ran a few worst-case scenarios through my head, then stopped packing, sat down on the bed and in Vietnamese and English began to tell the story of Hanh. The Vietnamese love a story, and amazingly, they both listened. When I finished, the guard said a few words and then left. I asked the manager what he was doing but he only shook his head as he left the room behind the guard.

I called Lady but couldn't reach her, then tried Thieu but his phone was down. At 8:45 A.M. there was another knock, more like a pounding this time, at my door. Without a moment's hesitation and without any forethought that I can recall now, I instinctively climbed into the armoire and held my breath. I almost laughed at myself. I couldn't believe I was doing what I was doing. I heard a key in my door, then someone came into the room. Almost immediately the door of the armoire was opened and I saw the remarkably staid expression of the hotel manager staring at me. He was accompanied again by the immigration guard and they'd been joined by another man. I could tell by the new-comer's uniform that he was an officer. I climbed out of the armoire. I remember now that I was amazed by how unfazed those three men seemed by my actions. They had just witnessed an unshaven, badly shaken forty-five-year-old American climb-ing out of an armoire, where he had been hiding to escape being escorted from their country, and it was as if they saw such things on a regular basis. Once I'd climbed out to confront them, they made absolutely no reference to it.

Before they began to speak, I asked the officer if I could please talk to him. He spoke gruffly to the hotel manager, who inter-preted, "The captain says there is no time to talk. That you must leave now."

"OK," I said, "I'll leave, but ask him if he would listen for just a few minutes. Tell him I've come over twelve thousand miles to be here. Tell him I love Vietnam. I want only five minutes and then I'll leave."

The manager hadn't finished translating when the Captain said "No," and then "No" again. He was serious and I tried to measure his seriousness. I tried to see how deeply felt it was and if it came from his heart or from his fear of not carrying out the order to escort me to the airport.

I held my hands out in front of me towards him, bringing my wrists together as though handcuffed.

"Arrest me," I said. "Take me to jail because I'm not leaving the hotel unless he gives me five minutes."

I had nothing to lose now. I actually hoped he would arrest me because then, at least, I would still be in Vietnam. I looked at the Captain's face after the manager had translated what I'd said and felt sorry for how I imagined he felt. I knew he had never been told no before. No one had ever resisted like I was resisting, especially not an American. He took his hat off and could not help expressing his utter exasperation. He looked at his watch, said something to the first guard who'd come to get me, and sent him out of the room.

In English, he said, "Five minutes."

I sat down on the bed and pulled him to sit beside me. I showed him the picture of Hanh. The manager interpreted. His English was good but I knew that he too was angry at me for resisting so I worried that he would somehow misrepresent what I was saying. I turned to him now.

"This is the most important thing to me in my life now," I told him. "I want you to please try very hard to get what I say right. I don't want to hear you make any mistakes."

He'd heard me speak some bad Vietnamese so I didn't know if he realized I was bluffing, but I could tell that I'd reached him, if only through fear.

I turned back to the Captain and told him the story of Hanh as he looked at her pictures. I knew I had to be brief so I chose only the most important phrases. After I made sure he understood that I'd come to Vietnam to adopt an orphaned eight-year-old girl from Binh Luc, I paused for a moment and asked him if he had any questions. He didn't answer.

"Are you married?" I asked.

"Yes," he said.

"Do you have children?"

"Yes."

"Do you have a daughter?"

"Yes," he said, clearly growing more impatient, "two daughters."

"Do you love them?"

He sat up straight and looked indignant. "Yes," he said, "of course."

"Would you do anything to help your daughters?"

"Yes," he said, almost spitting out the word.

"So would I," I said. "I would do anything for my daughter Nguyen Thi Hanh. I would travel twelve thousand miles for her, and come into Vietnam with a bad visa and stay in the Noi Ba Hotel. I would go to jail for her," I told him. "I would lie myself down on the runway across the street and not move if I thought it would keep me in Vietnam for only a second longer. She's waiting for me," I said. "If you send me away now I may never be able to reach her again. She knows I'm here. She has no father. I am her only hope. Like you," I said, "I'll do anything for my daughter."

He said nothing but shook his head and sighed what I wanted to believe sounded like resignation. He made three short, very animated phone calls, then told me I could stay for the rest of that day but only if I agreed to leave the next morning. I thanked him and lied that I would leave by tomorrow if my visa problems were not solved by then. He shook his head again and left with the hotel manager.

I couldn't keep myself from smiling, or from feeling what amounted to a perverse pleasure from having just rocked the Marxist/Leninist bureaucracy back on its heels simply by saying no and by telling the officer the story of Nguyen Thi Hanh. I lay down, closed my eyes and dozed off again.

51

Again the phone woke me. This time it was Thieu and I could tell immediately by his tone that things weren't good. Before he could explain what was going on I told him the story of the immigration guard coming for me and then leaving and then coming back with his captain. I told him how they had agreed to let me stay another day.

He said he was surprised, that he'd heard I would be leaving. He said he thought he might even miss me with this call. Then there was nothing and I thought for a moment that we'd been cut off. I said his name a few times and then I heard him very quietly say, "Yes, I'm here."

"I'm so sorry," he said. He said he had some very bad news for me. He and Duat had tried everything but it didn't look as if they would be able to get me a visa. He explained that it was difficult because I had come into the country on one kind of visa, a tourist visa, issued primarily for the purpose of the adoption, and the Writers' Association had no authority to issue me a working visa. He said that I had to return to the U.S. and apply for another visa, then return to Vietnam as a guest of the Writers' Association as I'd done in the past.

I could only manage a moan in response.

"I'm so sorry," he continued, "but there are more problems."

He told me that because of my current visa problem, because I'd come into Vietnam illegally on an expired passport, it would be best if I waited for some time before applying for a new visa. He said I should wait at least six months. I let him finish talking. I waited until the silence returned.

"No," I said, "you can't give up yet. I'm begging you, Thieu, to not give up." I asked him to call the Hanoi office of Holt, our adoption agency, and to call the U.S. embassy and to call Duat and ask him to call General Giap. Without hesitation he said that he would try to call me back.

I waited in the room. I was afraid that if I left I'd miss his call. I was too afraid to use the phone even to order something to eat. An hour later Thieu called back. He said that they were trying to work through the Provincial offices in Nam Ha, the province where the orphanage was located. He added that time was very short now and that the immigration officer at the airport was getting upset about my presence there. He said that I'd definitely have to leave tomorrow if nothing happened with Nam Ha. I didn't want to keep him on the phone long. I thanked him and told him that I had faith in him, that I knew he could help.

As soon as I hung up I went downstairs for something to eat. After the kidney stone and all the vomiting, my stomach was empty. I was exhausted and had eaten barely anything during the last twenty-four hours. I had to stay as strong as possible. If Thieu somehow did manage to get my visa, it would mean only the beginning of my journey. I would still have to travel to Binh Luc and spend another ten days or so in Hanoi processing Hanh's passport and exit visa, then another week in Bangkok to clear American immigration. After that we'd have twenty-four hours in the air before reaching JFK Airport.

As I walked back to my room I heard the phone ringing from the hall. I ran the last few feet and managed to reach the phone while it was still ringing. I heard Thieu's sad voice.

"Bad news again," he said. "It's too late for Nam Ha to help."

They said I should return to the U.S., get a new visa and begin the adoption process again.

I gave up then. I was too weary to go on and I could hear in Thieu's voice that there was nothing else he could do. I felt I'd already asked too much of him so I told him not to worry. I tried to mask the absolute defeat I felt come over me. I told him I'd call Jean to try to make my return travel reservations so at least I wouldn't have to fly to Singapore, at least I'd have control over my travel. I told him I'd be back as soon as I could and I thanked him and asked him to thank Lady and Duat. I told him that since I didn't have to leave until tomorrow morning, it would be nice if they could come out to the hotel and have dinner with me. I would understand, I said, if that wasn't possible. They'd already spent so much time trying to help. I knew they had their own work to do, their own lives to attend to.

"I want to try one more thing," Thieu said in response to my dinner invitation. He told me not to call Jean to make the return arrangements until I heard from him again. I told him I'd wait, and hung up, but I'd already resigned myself to leaving. I was surprised by the suddenness of my defeat. After so much effort and worry and pain, after so many conversations and nearly missed connections, I hadn't expected the end to come down so hard and so fast. I sat down and wrote a long fax to Jean that I'd have Thieu send to State College, telling her the whole long, sad story that I knew I wouldn't have the strength to tell her on the phone.

I spent the rest of the afternoon and evening drinking beer and falling in and out of fitful sleep tangled with dreams I couldn't seem to run from. I woke at six the next morning in that timeless daze that comes from bad sleep and from sorrow.

I spent the next half hour repacking and reorganizing my bags. I planned to leave the large suitcase that I'd filled with gifts for the orphanage staff and the children with Lady Borton so I could bring more things if I ever managed to come back. I felt an overwhelming sense of loss and despair. Already I began to dread the long flight back, alone, without Nguyen Thi Hanh. I dreaded the airport bus ride from JFK to La Guardia. I dreaded the flight from New York to Harrisburg and then the drive from Harrisburg to State College. I dreaded the thought of facing everyone at home and having to explain why I was alone. Most of all I dreaded the thought of the orphanage officials telling Nguyen Thi Hanh that I wouldn't be coming for her. I tried to imagine my return trip but couldn't. I simply could not envision a single image that would allow me to believe it would be possible to do it all again.

Just as I'd gotten my bags in order and finished writing notes to Lady and to Sylvia, the Holt representative in Hanoi, there was a knock at my door. I didn't care anymore. I wouldn't make any more desperate calls, although I was surprised I hadn't heard anything from Thieu. It occurred to me that he was too sad to call me with news of yet another failed attempt. I opened the door to the hotel manager. He had an odd smile on his face that pissed me off because it was a smile that seemed to say *See, I told you you'd have to leave.*

"You'll have to leave for the airport now," he said.

"No shit," I said. "Tell me something I don't know."

I hadn't even bothered to call Jean to make return flight arrangements. I guessed there was probably another flight to Singapore. I told him I was almost ready to leave and began gathering up my things.

The manager looked surprised and said an emphatic *No* in English. "You must leave for the airport immediately," he said. "You must leave your bags here for now." He began to explain further but was interrupted by the telephone. It was Thieu. Immediately I could tell that something in his voice was different, a lightness that I hadn't heard during the last two days.

"Good news," he said. He told me that they'd secured a new visa. He said he was getting ready to leave Hanoi to pick me up and take me to the airport, where the visa would be issued, and then bring me back to Hanoi. I told him the airport manager was in my room at that moment, waiting for me to leave. Thieu told me to give the phone to the manager.

After a few minutes of animated conversation with Thieu, the manager hung up. He looked even more serious than the first time he'd come for me.

"You must leave now," he said.

I couldn't believe what I was hearing. "Didn't Nguyen Quang Thieu just tell you that they have my visa?" I asked. I tried to explain that Thieu had just told me he was on his way to pick me up and take me to the airport to get my visa and then take me into Hanoi. I told him it was OK now, that I could stay. I must have looked half-mad with panic because he laughed out loud then and said he knew all of this. He said that the immigration office at the airport had just called him with the same news and that they had instructed him to bring me to the airport immediately. I could hardly believe what I was hearing. My heart wanted to fly out of my chest.

"Leave your bags and your friend will come for you here," he said.

After the short walk across the street to the airport I was greeted inside the processing area by the same captain and his officers who had come for me earlier. They were all smiling. I looked around the airport, which was mostly empty now. The immigration guards and others who worked in the airport were all apparently aware of my new status and everyone seemed to be smiling as I passed them in the airport on my way back to the immigration office. On the way the Captain apologized in Vietnamese for my difficulties. He said that someone in the Writers' Association had secured a new visa for me, good until the end of November.

Inside the immigration office I signed a few forms and the Captain handed me my passport, opened to an unbelievably beautiful Vietnamese visa stamped inside. He shook my hand. I asked him what I should do now and he looked puzzled. I asked again in Vietnamese and he smiled and said, "Finished!" and "*Di! Di!* Go! Go!"

Given the difficulties of the past forty-eight hours I was still wary. I looked around and then towards the door and began walking out. I half expected someone to grab me and tell me to stop, but I walked past the security gate without showing my visa, and out the door. No one grabbed me. A few of the guards waved a friendly good-bye. They were happy for me. I walked out the door into the late morning sun. Across the street I could see Thieu and Duat standing next to a car pulled up in front of the Noi Ba Hotel. They waved and smiled when they saw me. *Most amazing world,* I thought. *Most strange and most wonderful.*

52

Because of the newly built superhighway between the airport and Hanoi, a trip that had taken two hours in 1986 now took only fifteen minutes. As we drove into the outskirts of the city I immediately lost my way. I thought I knew it well. I'd spent hours purposefully getting myself lost in every section of Hanoi so that I could learn my way out and around. It had only been two years since my last visit, but the landscape and the cityscape were clearly and dramatically different. The prosperity that the mixed economy brought had already begun to have a huge impact on the city. Money was involved—billions of dollars of foreign investment. More money meant more hotels and restaurants and shops, and of course it meant more and more foreign business. Already the Japanese were ravaging the forests in the North.

For me to long for the old days of Hanoi was stupid and selfish and sentimental, I knew, though I still loved Hanoi best the way it looked and felt in 1986, and I loved how its people moved through the city. It was stupid to think of how things used to be because in 1986 there was not enough food, and little medicine. Thousands of children starved to death or died from simple dysentery that Kaopectate could have cured. Hovering over this grim postwar poverty was the heavy hand of Marxist/Leninist opportunism that had emerged most fully after the death of Ho Chi Minh, wanting to control practically every aspect of everyone's life. In postwar countries of victory like Vietnam, the generals live long and prosper. The Party revels almost giddily and pathologically in the success of its policies and doctrines, however little they contributed to the achievement of ordinary men and women's fighting all over the North and South, for their lives and for the simple ground they occupied with their families.

In 1986, when dusk came the city was mostly dark. A French-era gas streetlight or two flickered here and there, and a dim light leaked from the windows and cracked doorways of the houses of the poor. There were also a few lights in small street-side cafés and some small lanterns blinking around the perimeter of the lake on Nguyen Du beside tiny stands where women squatted in that particular Vietnamese way, selling their few packs of cigarettes, their few bottles of warm beer. I remember that lovers lingered there too, in those days, among tangled banyan trees. I would watch them nuzzle each other and coo and laugh for the minutes stolen from their crowded family houses until they would walk away, into the evening's desire.

Now, even miles from the heart of the city, I could see the light rising up from what I knew was the center of Hanoi, the old darkness gone now in the glare. The children have enough food now, most of them. There's modern medicine and nuclear microscopes and hydraulic postmodern prostheses for the tens of thousands of war-injured. The children are beautiful and confident and so smart that you want to love them all. They are bored with talk of the war and they will tell you so. They want to know about the world. They say that they love America. America is best, they say. Many, now, don't remember the dark time after the war. They don't remember the time of no rice. Secretly they laugh in that particularly sweet Vietnamese way at their parents, whom they love.

The Circle of Hanh

As we enter the heart of Hanoi, the streets are thick with cars, trucks, motorcycles, cyclos and bicycles. Mostly I notice the cars: two or three times more than my last trip, it seems. Some streets have even been widened to fit more cars, so the sidewalks that were once wide enough for promenade, as the French helped build them, were now narrow.

I had walked many times years before with a woman who, as a child, hid in the mountains north of Hanoi to escape Nixon's Christmas bombing in 1972. I met Yen first in 1986, and though we were drawn to each other for reasons I don't understand or even care to wonder about, it was difficult then even to be with each other publicly; and to visit with her privately at her home or in my room in the Party's guest house was forbidden by Vietnamese law. Before the Open Door policy reached its most inclusive and liberal stage, all Vietnamese were required by law to report to their local police any contact with foreigners, especially Americans. Our first few times together in 1986, and then again in 1990 when things had begun to open up more, were made more awkward too by the language barrier: I spoke and understood only a few words of Vietnamese, and though Yen spoke French it was still too early for her to have studied English. Still, after our first few hours together I knew we were meant to be friends, and I would come to spend time with her in her small house in the heart of old Hanoi, where she lived with her mother, father, her married sister, her brother-in-law and their two children. We would eventually spend time together all over the city, which she knew well enough to show me places no one else had.

The first evening with Yen stays with me because it was the first time I felt I had begun to move inside the country, inside its lives. I was at the end of a month long stay in Hanoi and I would leave the next morning for Bangkok. I was staying with a group of other American veterans who had also become writers and with a group of poets and novelists from Hanoi. I had met Yen three days before at a writers' conference, but because of a mistake I'd made when she'd given me her address, I wasn't able to find her. Few private homes had telephones in those days, and many of the streets were unmarked, with houses whose numbers had long ago disappeared.

In the afternoon of that last day in Vietnam I had been driven from the Party's guest house on West Lake a few kilometers from the city into the old section to do my last shopping. I knew Yen lived nearby but I felt hopelessly inept at finding her, or even my own way back. In the middle of the shopping day on a crowded street of metal pans and pots I turned around suddenly towards what I thought was the sound of my name barely rising above the hubbub and saw Yen standing a few feet away—only she wasn't looking at me; she hadn't seen me. I called her name and she looked up, smiling but not surprised, as if there had never been any doubt in her mind that we would see each other again. Perhaps because of their long years of war, the Vietnamese have learned somehow to wait months and even years for things to weave and twist away, then come back into the natural course of their lives.

We struggled to talk in the middle of the crowded marketplace, but we managed to make plans for me to come back into old Hanoi later in the evening after Yen had finished work. We would eat *pho* at a restaurant, she said; I would meet her family. She pointed in the direction of her house, which was nearby, and wrote the number on a piece of paper and stuck it in my shirt pocket. She shook my hand and smiled when we said good-bye.

That night, through a slow but soaking rain, I followed the abandoned trolley tracks to Hung Dao Street, where Yen lived, and I will never forget the evening that followed.

Miss Huang Yen sat down with me in the small tiled room of her family house where first we shared a glass of cold, sweet water. Later her mother brought us cake on a blue plate. She smiled at me when she turned to leave, and I saw that her teeth were stained ebony black from the betel nuts she chewed. I did not feel strange in that house that my country had tried to bomb into dust. I sat down with Yen on the floor of her room. She showed me photographs of her friends and of the places she had visited as a journalist. I felt as if she were pointing me towards something she thought I needed to know, and not long afterwards in English thick and dazed as blood, she told me how she had watched our planes move like monsters across the sky of her childhood. She told me how all the children of Hanoi had been taken in darkness to mountain hamlets.

She let me hold her hand, her shy and unmoving fingers, and she told me how afraid she was those days, and how that fear had dug inside her like a worm and lives inside her still. Yet she also tried to comfort me, because she is stronger. She said that I wasn't to blame and in her eyes I saw the million sorrows.

Much later, with pink light streaking through the clouds and early shoppers and peasants already on their way to the business of their lives, I tried to say good-bye outside on Hung Dao Street. I held her hand too long, so she looked back through the traffic and with her eyes told me I should leave.

Back at the guest house I ached for all the rest of that morning for Yen and for myself and nothing I could think or pray would make the ache stop. Some birds sang morning home across the lake. In small reed boats the lotus gatherers sailed out into their resuming white blossoms.

The Circle of Hanh

Yen and I had become friends in a way I'd never been friends with a woman before, and it was a friendship inextricable from the life I could feel beating inside the city. During our time together we would hold hands sometimes and she would say, "Walk with me as a friend."

We would walk down Nguyen Du Street beside the lake. We would follow the lost trolley tracks back into old Hanoi. I wanted to try to find the ancient gates. I imagined we could save at least their memory.

⟨◌⟩

As Thieu's car made its way through the crowded streets, I could see that the slower pace encouraged by the wide sidewalks and narrow streets of the past was changing before me. I don't know what we lose when we move too quickly through our lives, but I know that loss is great.

We pulled up in front of the hotel on Mai Hac De where I usually stayed. It was a magic location. Around the corner was a street famous for the *pho* made and served there, and I liked the people in the neighborhood: fiercely independent and wonderfully curious. The hotel is also near the offices of my writer and editor friends. I checked in quickly, happy to see some familiar faces of the men and women working in the small hotel, who also seemed happy to see me. They knew why I was in the country this time and they were all very pleased about it. Mai, the night manager, told me that she would help me care for my daughter during my stay in Hanoi. She said it was a good thing that I was doing and that I must be a very kind man.

I dropped my bags off in my room and left again for dinner with Lady Borton and Thieu. I knew I needed to slow down after the previous forty-eight hours, but I also had no time; the next morning I would drive out to Binh Luc, Nam Ha Province, with Lady Borton and the American and Vietnamese representatives from Holt, our adoption agency in Hanoi, to meet my daughter Nguyen Thi Hanh, eight years old.

Tonight I wanted to drink with my friends in what had become the second city of my heart and to let the shots of American scotch and the glasses of Vietnamese beer warm me into a diminished feeling of things, and to sit down to one of those long and drowsy meals I had come to look forward to in Hanoi. I grew up eating at the tables of Yugoslavs in Lorain, Ohio, and except for them, I would rather eat with Vietnamese than with anyone else. In both places, I love most the pace of the meal, the way the good talk of friendship and of family is woven and flows through the eating and drinking so that it becomes a song, and how everyone has a chance to tell his or her story. I love the rise and fall of those unhurried voices, and the sound the beer makes poured generously into glasses. Although we had finished our work for the day, we practiced at that table in Hanoi, and at many like it before, the study of ritual and of lingering anticipation. Here I learned another kind of music of the heart.

We ate whole steamed fish and rice, Thieu generously offering me one of the fish's baked, cloudy-white eyeballs that the Vietnamese relish for its taste and for the luck they believe it will bring. I was happy to accept. I took it up with my chopstick, dipped it long in *nuoc mam,* the pungent, fermented fish sauce that is a staple on every Vietnamese table, and then chewed it slowly, much to Thieu's delight. Lady Borton declined the other eye so Thieu took his turn.

"Tomorrow," he said, "we will both be smarter because of eating the fish's eyes. We will see into things."

I needed that. "I would be much more at ease about the adoption if I could see into things like the fish," I said.

We talked for a few more minutes about our plans to drive to Binh Luc the next morning, I thanked Lady and Thieu again for their miraculous help and we toasted with one more American scotch whiskey the new life Nguyen Thi Hanh and I would begin in less than eight hours. Fatigue was gradually wearing away at my excitement at having made it to Hanoi. The meal and the drinks began to dull me pleasantly. We left the restaurant and on the street I told Lady and Thieu that I wanted to walk back to the hotel to clear my head a bit and to see some of Hanoi on what would be my last evening alone here, and we said our good-byes.

I was carried off into the human traffic where I felt at ease and at peace. As it always is when I'm in Hanoi, I can hardly walk a few blocks before someone speaks to me, a sweet-faced school-child, a woman shopkeeper, even old men still wearing remnants of their North Vietnamese Army uniforms.

They call out the word *American* to me as I pass, wanting to engage in whatever English conversation they can manage.

"*Vung,*" I say in return so that I can practice my Vietnamese, "*Toi my.*" Yes, I am an American, and always they smile at this and they lie that my accent is good, but they don't want to speak Vietnamese; they want to practice their English, the most accomplished among them interested especially in learning slang and idiosyncratic phrases and words.

"*Toi noi khong muon noi tiang anh,*" I say. I don't want to speak English.

"*Toi muon noi tiang Viet tai sau toi tich Vietnam.*" I want to speak Vietnamese because I love Vietnam.

There is little else that you can say as a foreigner, especially an American, to a Vietnamese man, woman or child in Hanoi that is more delightful to them. Most Vietnamese with whom I have at least a passing relationship almost always respond the same way when I say that I love their country. They pause for a long moment and look hard into my eyes. It must sound strange to them, given our not-so-distant past. It sounds strange to me too, but it feels good and true to say it.

In 1986, during my first trip to Hanoi, hardly anyone spoke English and I knew only a few words in Vietnamese that I struggled to pronounce. In those days, when the so-called Open Door policy was just beginning to make some differences in people's lives, it was still unusual to even see an American. The generation of men and women in their sixties and seventies spoke French if they spoke anything other than Vietnamese, and the children spoke Russian, grudgingly.

Today almost everyone speaks a few words of English and most people who live in the city come home to a late dinner after a long workday and then head out again at night for their private English-language classes.

I walked in the direction of my hotel, which was less than a kilometer away, but still I managed to get lost and stayed lost longer than I wanted to. I finally made my way back by following a series of complicated and sometimes completely ambiguous directions I got from people along the way. I didn't even undress before I stretched out on the bed to rest for a few minutes before getting ready for the next morning's trip to Binh Luc. I closed my eyes and fixed my tired brain on the sound of the ceiling fan, its awkward rhythm soothing me.

53

I don't remember falling asleep that night, but I know I did, so deeply that I didn't wake fully until I found myself inside a van in the morning dark, being driven to the village where my daughter waited in the orphanage. I was happy deep inside a place I did not know my body had. I also felt on the verge of losing my grip on things: I was driven by something out of my control, moving inside some kind of zone, almost mindlessly exerting more and more self-control so that I could accomplish what had almost seemed impossible only a day earlier.

I closed my eyes to the chatter in the car and tried to imagine Nguyen Thi Hanh. I had spent a lot of time during the previous few months looking at pictures of her and reading about her life and about how she had come to be where she was. Jean and I had learned from the adoption agency very early on that Holt didn't simply give Vietnamese children to adoptive American parents just because ours is the land of plenty. Instead they try carefully to match children with parents. They look inside the lives. We learned too that at every juncture the prospective adoptive child has full veto power over any family without fear of jeopardizing his or her chances for a future adoption. We had been required to assemble an exhaustive dossier of dozens of documents in their original or in the form of a certified and notarized copy, as well as background checks, police reports, two home study reports, interview notes from social workers, letters of recommendation, Vietnamese legal documents, contracts of promise of care, signed concessions to certain Vietnamese laws, complete income statements, two-thousand-word personal narratives, a complete history of both of our families, a history of our marriage and of our fifteen years as parents of our son, academic credentials, medical reports, personal religious narratives and a carefully designed portfolio of fifty-five photographs of our extended families, our house and cars, our place of work, the school our son attended and a few shots of the center of our community, all of which had to be mounted on "brightly colored paper" and copiously annotated, and all of which consisted of a series of designated poses such as Mother with Father; Mother with son; Father with son; Father with house; Mother and Father with car; etcetera, etcetera, etcetera, for fifty-five poses.

Working almost full-time, it took us months to assemble the dossier. It had seemed impossible to me then. The dossier requirements were almost enough to make me have my first serious doubts about the whole idea, but Jean was a force that confronted the mountain of empty forms with a frenzied grace; nothing slipped by her or discouraged her until every last blank space had been filled in and every date and signature accounted for and every onion-skin-thin piece of paper was in its proper place. Without her strength in managing that enormous and essential task, we never would have succeeded.

I felt I had come to know Nguyen Thi Hanh, if only a little. At night in my bed in Pennsylvania in the weeks before my departure, I would lie on my back with my eyes closed, exhausted and sleepless at the same time, and her spirit would sometimes come alive inside my head. Some nights when it seemed that no progress had been made for months and that the adoption was only a dream, I could feel a life beating there.

The Circle of Hanh

Nguyen Thi Hanh had spent the last few months learning about us as well. Once we had finished the dossier, it was taken to Hanoi by Holt, processed through the rigorously convoluted socialist bureaucracy and tediously translated into Vietnamese. All of the personal documents and narratives were shown to Nguyen Thi Hanh while the Vietnamese social worker from Holt tried to conjure for her an image of our lives that she could manage. After they went carefully through the dossier, Nguyen Thi Hanh talked for a long time with Luu Thi Hong Van, the director of the orphanage (whom Hanh called *Me,* or mother), with provincial and district officials, and with Holt's Vietnamese social worker so she could decide if she would "choose" us for her family. She did choose us, and we got word that she had told them she was very pleased that her mother was a painter and her father a poet; she was pleased too that she would now have a big brother, and two cats, that she would walk to her school. She said she thought the picture of her school was very beautiful.

More than I had imagined was possible, we had learned about each other before I went to Vietnam, but as I traveled through the country towards the orphanage, I realized more and more deeply that I did not know what to expect. How could I? This was the country I had invaded as a boy. These were the people I had helped bring to grief, and now one of their children would be coming home with me to be my daughter in another world.

Outside I could see that the landscape was changing as we neared Binh Luc. The valley began to widen and spread its degrees of green outwards towards the sea. There were only a few scattered small houses, but everywhere there was rice and the people who worked the rice. This was the landscape of my daughter's life and I could feel her more strongly as I realized that.

The Circle of Hanh

The Vietnamese Holt representative smiled at me and began to speak nervously in English about what lay ahead for me today. She switched to Vietnamese then, and with Lady Borton interpreting, began to brief me about how careful I had to be in responding to the many subtle cues I would get from the district and provincial officials as we made our way through the bureaucracy that baffled even the Vietnamese. There would be many tests, she said, and it was important that I do and say the right things at the right times.

In English, Lam reminded me that at the ceremony where I would officially accept Hanh as my daughter, I also had to say something in Vietnamese. I had known about this part for a month or so and I had written and practiced a short speech in Vietnamese over and over to myself, and to Giang Nong, my Vietnamese friend from Hanoi who studies at my university, and to anyone who would listen until I thought I had it right. Although I had studied Vietnamese on and off for nearly five years, mostly on my own and during several brief language lessons during my trips to Hanoi, I worried about saying something that would embarrass Hanh. Because Vietnamese is, among other things, a tonal language, it is therefore amazingly easy for a nonnative speaker to say something stupid simply by dropping a tone instead of rising with it.

In the van I said the speech out loud for those I knew would be my harshest critics. They laughed and applauded when I finished. Lady Borton, whose Vietnamese is almost native—idiosyncratic and finely tuned to its complicated contextual nature—made a few corrections and revisions, including how, when I spoke to Nguyen Thi Hanh, I should try not to refer to myself using the more formal pronoun, *toi,* but instead use the more familiar *Bó,* or father, so that Hanh would know immediately what my intentions were. These seemingly minor details, when ignored, can have a profound effect on any kind of interaction with the Vietnamese, and I was once again grateful for Lady's help and for her skills.

Although the Holt people wouldn't say so, I knew from other friends in Hanoi that these adoptions sometimes didn't work. Sometimes they inexplicably broke down, even after the parents had come into Vietnam for their child and had stayed for months at a time, exhausting all of their resources until finally they would have to give up and leave. Somewhere along the baffling trail of checks and counterchecks someone would see something he or she didn't like and pull the plug; that is, they would lay the dossier in its own place on an unoccupied desk covered with other dossiers. No decisions would be made. The Vietnamese don't like to say the word *no*. They simply say nothing at all when they can't or won't say *yes*. One must learn quickly that in practically every aspect of Vietnamese life, the lack of a response to a question or a request means no. I had heard those stories, and I could sense that the Holt people had them in mind as we got close to Binh Luc, so I tried to make them laugh.

I tried in Vietnamese to make up a *ca dao,* a traditional oral folk poem. I made a rhyme using the words *nuoc mam* (fish sauce) and *Lam,* the name of the beautiful Vietnamese woman who worked for Holt and was traveling with us today. Everyone laughed loudly at the same time when I said it, so I immediately said it again, and they laughed harder. I worked on my *ca dao* out loud for the next five minutes or so until it consisted entirely of lines ending with either *nuoc mam* or *Lam.* With every new version my friends laughed harder, and I laughed with them. The enabling and un-forgettable laughter of release that filled the van lifted me up into happiness, carrying me along.

I was tumbling inside the realm of that laughter when I felt the van lurch to one side suddenly. I looked out of the window and saw that we had pulled off the road onto a grassy path and that we were moving through the crumbling brick gates of the orphanage. I realized just then that in spite of everything I had done to ready myself for this moment, I was woefully unprepared. My body began to shake and I felt cold even in the heat of the northern autumn. The van pulled up next to another brick entryway that framed a small building. Immediately we were surrounded by children who had been waiting all day for us. Someone slid the van's door open to their smiling faces and I got out slowly, trying to find the one face I knew. The Holt people were greeting the representatives from the orphanage, motioning for me to join them too, when I saw her just beyond the second gate, squatting in that particular Vietnamese way at the edge of their fishpond, dragging a long stick across the surface of the water and trying very hard to ignore our presence.

I held her in my eyes and I thought about the stories I had told the immigration officials when they had come to take me to the airport to leave the country. I thought about how strong I had felt throughout that struggle because of the clarity of my purpose. I had convinced myself along the way that I would do or say or endure whatever it took to see the adoption through, and now as I looked at Nguyen Thi Hanh across the dusty sun-streaked courtyard of my imaginings, I felt the full force of the river of love that had finally run its course and carried me here.

I greeted and shook hands with the orphanage officials and quickly turned back towards the fishpond. Nguyen Thi Hanh had not yet turned to look in our direction. I glanced over at Lady. I didn't have to ask the question because she knew what I was thinking, and she nodded for me to go. I took a few steps towards the pond where Hanh squatted and from a few yards away I called out *Chau con gai bo,* Hello, father's daughter.

The Circle of Hanh

Hanh stood up suddenly and whirled around to look at me. I was squatting now; in her presence I felt uncomfortably large and I worried that my size would frighten her so I did what I could to look smaller. When she saw me she covered what was trying to be a smile with her hands and then ran away, into the arms of Van, the director, standing nearby with Lady. I didn't get up to follow her. I did something right for once. I told myself that I would not try to hold on to her or to pull her towards me or to be more than I was to her on this first day. I vowed to myself that very moment that no matter how powerfully I felt drawn to pick her up and kiss her face and take her into my heart, I would not move towards her until she was ready. I would follow her lead. I would be there for her, but only on her terms.

After tea and a brief introductory ceremony in the orphanage's small reception area, we got back in the van, joined now by Van, with Hanh on her lap because there were no empty seats. I sat behind Van and I could see Hanh's face. We caught each other's eyes a few times as she let herself be more curious in her gaze. In Vietnamese I told her that her mother and her brother were very happy that she was coming and that they were waiting for her in America. Hanh looked up at Van and made a face and laughed quietly. It was my accent, I knew, and the simple pleasure she got from hearing me speak her language, however clumsily.

We were all swept up then into a long, frantic afternoon of meetings and ceremonies at several different provincial and district offices. More than once along the way a small snag would develop because our timing was off according to one official or another. The snag would always be followed by much animated talk and by the sound of voices rising almost too high in their insistence. I didn't worry over it. I was on autopilot by then. I was most alive, but I don't remember many of the details. I signed a hundred documents, shook hands and thanked the cool officials, and near what I knew was the end of the official drama, I gave my speech in Vietnamese. Lam and Lady Borton had advised me well. I don't even know if I said what I had written and practiced. I don't know if I mangled the simple Vietnamese sentences or if I said them at least clearly enough to be understood. I remember only that I stood up and opened my mouth, and the words seemed to come on their own as in a dream of an unlearned language. I know now that I could not have done better. As soon as I finished my speech and offered a toast to Vietnam and to the province of Nam Ha, famous for its rice and the violence of its weather, I knew that it was the one gesture from me that they had been waiting for, a gesture that they had expected but may have also doubted would ever come.

We finally all piled out of that last dreary office and drove a short distance into the village to a small open-air restaurant where four long tables had been pushed together and were already being covered with dishes of food and bottles of beer that two or three young women carried out from the kitchen. I wanted to sit next to Hanh, to use the occasion of the lunch to speak with her, but I could tell that she was still very shy of me. She sat across the table from me, between Van and Lady, whom she had already embraced and with whom she laughed over something I couldn't understand. We all offered up more toasts, then settled into the meal.

I knew that Hanh was not accustomed to eating this way. The meal, paid for by Holt, was very special, and well beyond the means of most Vietnamese. Hanh stared wide-eyed at the dishes of every food she had probably ever seen or eaten, and some she probably had never seen, piling up on the table. After some initial hesitation, and at the urging of Van, who knew the value of eating as much as you could when the opportunity presented itself, Hanh began to eat. I had never seen a child eat that way before. I smiled to myself as I watched her. I could not imagine where, in that small body, all of that food was going, or how it could be contained there. She ate until the last plate of scraps was taken from the table. I watched her lean back into her chair, bend and stretch her back and then belch so loudly she made herself laugh. Van scolded her but could not resist laughing as well.

I still had not touched my daughter's hand, nor had Hanh said even a single word to me. I saw her climb up and whisper something into Van's ear. Van laughed and I heard her say *"Vung, vung,"* yes, yes.

Without quite looking into my face directly, Hanh leaned just a degree or so towards me and said *"Ca-mon Bo,"* Thank you, Father, then turned back to Van, laughing. It would be enough to sustain me for a long time, and I was suddenly glad about my decision that morning to hold back and let her make the way for us. I also felt something let go inside me when she spoke; a rope of nervousness and worry had been released by that simple sentence and I felt myself relax for the first time that day.

The rest happened too quickly, I think, for everyone. We drove the few kilometers back to the orphanage where I collected a small bundle of Hanh's clothes and an album of photographs of her friends and her teachers at the orphanage. I said good-bye to Van and promised I would try to care for Hanh as well as she had, and that Hanh would be my daughter as if she had been born into our family. When I addressed her I used the familiar pronoun *chi,* sister, for the first time, and she embraced me.

I turned to watch as, alone or in pairs, all of the children made their way to where Hanh stood next to Van and said their sweet and quiet good-byes. I looked hard at Hanh's face and I could see some panic in her eyes as our driver started the engine of the van and turned the air conditioner on for our drive back to Hanoi.

An impromptu group photograph of the children and staff of the orphanage standing around me in the courtyard was set up but interrupted by a sudden, heavy rain.

Van put her arms around Hanh then, and I saw that for the first time they were both crying. I wanted to tell Hanh that I loved her, because I did. I wanted to tell her that I wished she would come and be a part of our family more than anything else in the world, but that if she wanted to stay in Binh Luc, and not come home with me, I would understand, and I would love her just as much. I almost made the words come out of my mouth, but I had the sense for once to stay quiet.

Van let go of Hanh and then, looking up into the sky, she pushed her gently towards the van. Hanh immediately found Lady Borton in the backseat and sat beside her, and held on to her.

As we pulled away through the courtyard and the arched gate, I watched Hanh look back more than once. Many children were waving in the rain, their small hands through the distance like lotus blossoms on the fishpond, opening.

About the Author

Bruce Weigl was born in Lorain, Ohio, in 1949. He is the author of ten collections of poetry, most recently *Song of Napalm* (Atlantic Monthly Press, 1988), *What Saves Us* (TriQuarterly Books, 1992), *Sweet Lorain* (TriQuarterly Books, 1996), and *Archeology of the Circle* (Grove Press, 1999). Weigl is also the editor or coeditor of three collections of critical essays, most recently *Charles Simic: Essays on the Poetry* (University of Michigan Press, 1996), as well as an anthology of poetry, fiction and nonfiction, *Writing Between the Lines: An Anthology on War and Its Social Consequences,* coedited with Kevin Bowen (University of Massachusetts Press, 1997). In addition, Weigl has published three volumes of poetry in translation: *Poems from Captured Documents,* cotranslated from the Vietnamese with Thanh Nguyen (University of Massachusetts Press, 1994); *Mountain River: Vietnamese Poetry from the Wars: 1948– 1993,* coedited and cotranslated from the Vietnamese with Nguyen Ba Chung and Kevin Bowen (University of Massachusetts Press, 1998); and *Angel Riding a Beast,* poems by Liliana Ursu, cotranslated from the Romanian with the author (Northwestern University Press, 1998).

Weigl's poetry, translations, essays, articles, reviews and interviews have appeared in such magazines as *The Nation, TriQuarterly, Field, The Kenyon Review, The New Yorker, The New York Times, Western Humanities Review, American Poetry Review, The Southern*

Review, Ploughshares, The Paris Review, Antaeus and *Harper's.* In addition, his poems have been widely anthologized, most recently in *The Best American Poetry, 1994,* edited by A. R. Ammons and David Lehman; *The Morrow Anthology of Younger American Poets,* edited by Dave Smith and David Bottoms; *Poets of the '90s; Anthology of Modern War Literature,* edited by Paul Fussell; and *Against Forgetting: Twentieth-Century Poetry of Witness,* edited by Carolyn Forché. Weigl's poetry has been translated into Vietnamese, Chinese, Czech, German, Dutch, Spanish, Bulgarian, Romanian and Slovenian, and published internationally. For his work Weigl has twice been awarded the Pushcart Prize; a Patterson Poetry Prize; a prize from the Academy of American Poets; the Breadloaf Fellowship in Poetry; a Yaddo Foundation Fellowship; and a National Endowment for the Arts Grant for poetry. He is past president of the Associated Writing Programs.